GROWING
TRUE
DISCIPLES

BARNA REPORTS *for* HIGHLY EFFECTIVE CHURCHES

GROWING

TRUE

DISCIPLES

New Strategies for Producing

Genuine Followers of Christ

GEORGE BARNA

President, Barna Research Group, Ltd.

WATERBROOK
PRESS

GROWING TRUE DISCIPLES
PUBLISHED BY WATERBROOK PRESS
12265 Oracle Boulevard, Suite 200
Colorado Springs, Colorado 80921
A division of Random House, Inc.

All Scripture quotations, unless otherwise indicated, are taken from the *Holy Bible, New International Version*®. NIV®. Copyright © 1973, 1978, 1984 by International Bible Society. Used by permission of Zondervan Publishing House. All rights reserved.

ISBN 1-57856-423-9

Published in association with Sealy M. Yates, Literary Agent, Orange, California.

Library of Congress Cataloging-in-Publication Data
Barna, George.
    Growing true disciples : new strategies for producing genuine followers of
Christ / George Barna.— 1st ed.
        p. cm. — (Barna reports for highly effective churches series)
    Includes bibliographical references.
    ISBN 1-57856-423-9
        1. Discipling (Christianity) I. Title

BV4520 .B345 2001
253—dc21

                                                            2001045352

This book has been previously released by Issachar Resources under the same title in a slightly different version.

Printed in the United States of America
2005

10 9 8 7 6

CONTENTS

CHAPTER ONE

DO YOU WANT TO MAKE A DIFFERENCE?

Ignite people's passion for God
and get out of their way.

Christians and Christian churches employ all kinds of strategies to influence their world.

We try to elect politicians who share our values and goals.

We strive to enact laws and policies that reflect our beliefs.

We attempt to expose people to Christian ideas and precepts through religious radio and television programming.

We hope to shape the minds of young people by enrolling them in Christian schools or by ensuring that God and His principles are not completely removed from the public school environment.

We use clever advertising campaigns and comprehensive direct marketing programs to encourage people to attend our churches or to develop a relationship with God.

We endeavor to get people to know Jesus by inviting them to evangelistic crusades, revivals, or other outreach events.

All such efforts are well intentioned and bear some fruit. But I would like to propose what I believe is a better strategy for growing the kingdom of God.

IGNITE AND NURTURE PEOPLE'S PASSION FOR GOD

What would happen if we were to focus on the four out of every ten adults and one out of every three teenagers who have already asked Jesus Christ to be their Savior—and do everything we can to help them grow into inspired, unmistakable disciples of Jesus?

What would happen for God's kingdom if we did not consider our job complete when people confess their sins and say a prayer inviting Jesus to be their Redeemer, but would *use their new commitments to Christ as a launching pad for a lifelong quest to become individuals who are completely sold out—emotionally, intellectually, physically, spiritually—to the Son of God?*

Churches work hard at trying to expand and strengthen the kingdom of God with all types of creative and life-affecting ministries. Thousands of churches are currently fine-tuning their worship services to make them more attractive and compelling. The typical church labors to integrate numerous programs, classes, and other offerings into its menu of possibilities. Millions of dollars flow from church budgets into events each year in an effort to influence people's thinking and behavior. Literally billions of dollars are spent every year maintaining, upgrading, and expanding buildings and facilities to provide the space and equipment required for the ministries planned by the church. To appeal to people who have thus far turned a cold shoulder to God, churches and denominations launch sophisticated marketing campaigns that are designed to reposition churches and raise awareness of the things of God.

All of those activities can be justified by their intent and outcomes. But here's a better strategy: *Ignite people's passion for God and get out of their way.* When individuals are single-minded in their devotion to God, their commitment to His ways and His principles becomes much deeper, much more intense. Once they have made an enduring and serious commitment, the peripherals don't matter as much. They'll endure worship services that may not meet their exact specifications because their focus is on God, not themselves. They'll attend activities at times that are not optimally convenient because the most important reality is to experience God's presence. They will sacrifice more of their hard-earned money for the purposes of ministry because they recognize that they are stewards, not owners. They will gladly share their faith in Christ with nonbelievers because they understand their responsibility to other people and to God, and because they simply cannot contain their own excitement about the privilege of relating to God.

Redefining Ministry Success

When you talk to pastors, church staff, and lay leaders across the nation you quickly discover that churches work hard to increase attendance figures, to provide a full range of programs, and to have adequate facilities to support a broad-based, inclusive ministry. The people and resources available for such ministry efforts represent a tremendous blessing from God.

But what if we were to change our standards? Suppose we were to de-emphasize attendance statistics, square footage, and income figures in favor of a commitment to depth and authenticity in discipleship? What if we were to redefine ministry success in these ways:

- congregants who worship not just on Sundays but every day of the week—not just in the sanctuary but wherever they are

- constant efforts by the laity to discover new insights into their faith and to convert that information into personal application

- complete submission to the Holy Spirit in both decision making and behavior

- hearts that are sensitive to sin and wounded every time they do something that offends God

- individuals who joyfully share their resources—time, money, skills, information, relationships, possessions—with those in need, especially those who share a love of Christ and a commitment to His people

- a deep commitment to building a lasting and life-changing community among those who profess Jesus Christ as their Savior and Lord

- spontaneous demonstrations of selfless compassion toward those in need of emotional, physical, financial, or spiritual assistance

- engagement in "organic evangelism"—the process of sharing one's faith in Christ in very natural and unforced ways, based on relationships with the recipients of the information and supported by lifestyle modeling

- people who live differently from the norm because of their faith, leading lives that conform to the dictates of Scripture without cutting corners or trying to interpret biblical passages for personal comfort or advantage

- a church body that projects (and lives up to) an image of being loving, caring, focused, and clear-minded in its pursuit of the ways of God

- individuals who are continually linked to God through prayer and meditation, as if they were "online" twenty-four hours a day with the ultimate spiritual power

- believers who take the initiative to use their gifts, skills, and training for the benefit of their church without having to be cajoled into serving

Why would these outcomes constitute "success"? Because churches would be made up not merely of members but of *true disciples*—men, women, boys, and girls committed to Jesus Christ as Savior and Lord and growing daily in their knowledge, love, and service to Him. Churches would be bolstered by the ongoing efforts of lay leaders, and paid professionals would facilitate lay ministry instead of having to initiate and lead those efforts.

> *Not one of the adults we interviewed said that their goal in life was to be a committed follower of Jesus Christ or to make disciples.*

Most church leaders will nod their heads in approval and suggest that these are the very things they are striving to achieve in their church. In all honesty, though, few churches achieve these outcomes—largely because we're not really serious about them. If we were to redefine discipleship and truly invest in it, we could reach these laudable ends.

WHAT ARE WE ABOUT?

To pastors and church staff, *discipleship* is a tired word. To most laypeople, it is a meaningless word. But let's not get hung up on terminology for the moment. Let's get hung up on our failure to produce indefatigable imitators of Christ. Let's get motivated by our waning influence in the world. Let's commit to doing whatever it takes to reinvigorate the church so that it will honor God, help change lives, and take its rightful place as the primary agent of transformation in our culture.

Just moments before His ascent to heaven, our Lord Jesus Christ gave this final command:

> All authority in heaven and on earth has been given
> to me. Therefore go and make disciples of all
> nations, baptizing them in the name of the Father
> and of the Son and of the Holy Spirit, and teaching
> them to obey everything I have commanded you.
> And surely I am with you always, to the very end
> of the age. (Matthew 28:18-20)

The Great Commission gets our juices flowing, doesn't it? It's our marching orders from God. But how many Christians do you know whose articulated life purpose is to help fulfill that tremendous challenge? How many believers do you know who get out of bed every morning asking what they can do to show and tell people about Jesus, to make those people disciples of the Lord, and to act like true disciples themselves?

Here's a morsel of perspective. In one recent nationwide survey we asked people to describe their goals in life. Almost nine out of ten adults described themselves as "Christian." Four out of ten said they were personally committed to Jesus Christ, had confessed their sins, and believed they will go to heaven after they die because of God's grace provided through Jesus' death and resurrection. But not one of the adults we interviewed said that their goal in life was to be a committed follower of Jesus Christ or to make disciples. (This survey, by the way, included interviews with pastors and other church leaders as well as hundreds of people who regularly attend church services and programs.)

A PARADIGM SHIFT

I want to challenge you to rethink what discipleship means and what it looks like in your church. I hope that, as a result of reading this book, you will reevaluate how you disciple other people. I want you to reassess the nature of your own commitment to Christ—that is, your own spiritual growth. Toward that end, let me suggest that we will probably have to alter the ways in which we think about and practice discipleship. Here are some of the transitions you and your church may have to make in order to improve the quality of your disciple-making strategy:

- shift from program-driven ministry to people-driven ministry

- change from emphasis on building consensus to building character

- de-emphasize recalling Bible stories; emphasize applying biblical principles

- move from concern about quantity (people, programs, square footage, dollars) to concern about quality (commitment, wisdom, relationships, values, lifestyle)

- retool developmental ministry efforts from being unrelated and haphazard to being intentional and strategic

- replace ministry designed to convey knowledge with efforts intended to facilitate holistic ministry

- alter people's focus from feel-good activities to absolute commitment to personal growth, ministry, and authenticity in their faith

Maybe you have heard such challenges before and are no longer moved by calls for revitalization. In *Growing True Disciples* I will argue that unless we embrace a comprehensive and far-reaching commitment to radical change in how we conduct our lives and our ministries, we are doomed to minimal results. If we hope to make a significant difference in the lives of individuals and in the nation's culture, then we must improve our intentionality, our intensity, and our strategies.

An old leadership adage is relevant to our dilemma: The things that got us to where we are today will not get us to where we need to be tomorrow. Qualitative growth demands constant upgrading and intensifying of our efforts. Unless you are completely satisfied with the state of your personal spiritual life and the spiritual life of your congregation, you must accept both the need to improve and the paradigm shift that will facilitate such improvement. Doing more of what you're already doing won't take you to the next level. Doing more of the same and doing it better won't get you there either. In all likelihood you'll need to integrate new strategies and new tactics to climb to a higher plane of ministry impact and lifestyle purity.

> *The things that got us to where we are today*
> *will not get us to where we need to be tomorrow.*

The natural tendency, of course, is to believe that we are doing okay, that we just need to tweak a few things and everything will be great. If you find yourself leaning in that direction, read the list of seven transitions again. Those are not overnight, quick-fix upgrades. Reread the list of twelve lifestyle outcomes in the previous section of this chapter. Those are not likely to happen without some radical transitions in thinking and commitment.

It all starts with a clear sense of what you are striving to accomplish. Are you satisfied with the nature of your church today but simply want your church to be bigger? Or are you committed to seeing a qualitative improvement in the ministry of your church and in the lives of the individuals within it?

If you understand the magnitude of what we're discussing, then you realize shifting to an emphasis on growing true disciples is a major undertaking. Should we bother? Can't we just keep on going down the same path we're on, making incremental adjustments along the way?

No. I don't know how to state it more bluntly. The Christian church is failing to live up to its promise; we're not even coming close to fulfilling it. Our nation has a strong economy but a weak morality. People are more interested in faith and religion than in Jesus. Believers are largely indistinguishable from nonbelievers in how they think and live. The church has lost its place at the table of cultural influence. Can we restore the impact of the church through more events and buildings? No. It will take zealots for Christ—individuals who are intractably devoted to knowing, loving, and serving Him with all their heart, mind, strength, and soul—if we are to transform our world.

THE REASON FOR HOPE

Honestly, our society's only hope of moral restoration is for the church to fulfill its calling from God. He called it into being so that the world would be impacted by the thoughts, words, and deeds of His followers.

But can the church possibly live up to God's mighty calling? Absolutely! In fact, there are three persuasive reasons to believe that the church can fulfill God's lofty expectations.

First, we can look at the history of the church. Two thousand years ago Jesus turned the world upside down by ignoring politics and institutional leverage and gathering twelve losers around Himself. He prepared these men to infiltrate their culture with a life-giving message, a transformed lifestyle, and a burning desire to serve God with every ounce of capacity they possessed—or die in the process. It was an improbable strategy, but it worked. The passion of Jesus' disciples was contagious. Without buildings, budgets, programs, curricula, or mass media, they built the foundations for what has become the world's most prolific faith group. Can you think of any reason why the modern church cannot have as much or greater impact as that small band of early believers?

Second, we must consider the heart of God. He created humans for the purpose of knowing, loving, and serving Him. His specific command to us, delivered through His Son, is that we should develop communities of faith to facilitate the growth of our relationship with Him and our service to others. He equipped us for this task with special gifts and abilities and with enormous resources—most important, His Holy Spirit who lives within and works through us. He gave us a huge task, yes, but He gave us all we would ever need to accomplish the task. Endowed by the Creator with all the tools and resources required to shape the world into a God-fearing, worshiping community, Christians have no excuse for not mastering the challenge.

Third, let's not overlook one aspect of our culture that will enable us to make progress toward the desired outcome: the American can-do spirit. Americans love a good challenge. When posed with a possibility that seems just beyond our grasp but merits our energies, we often take up the cause and rise to the challenge. If God's people in the United States can understand what is at stake and be given a reasonable plan of attack, it seems likely that they would energetically pursue the potential to be the true church.

THREE COMMITMENTS

Recognize that reaching the level of excellence called for within the church will demand three commitments of us.

First, we must rely upon God. This is a battle we cannot win on our own strengths and abilities. We must lean heavily on His Word, His power, and His guidance.

Second, for the church to be the church He envisioned, we must commit to personal growth. That commitment intimates that we are willing to change in ways that may be uncomfortable or unexpected.

Third, we must recognize that the church is not a private, individual endeavor but a corporate venture. We must be willing to minimize ourselves for the good of the whole, using our abilities and resources in harmony with those of other believers for the benefit of the church at large.

THE PICTURE OF SUCCESS

What would success look like if the church were to be comprised of true followers of Christ? We need only return to a well-known passage of Scripture to be reminded of the product we seek to achieve:

> They devoted themselves to the apostles' teaching and to the fellowship, to the breaking of bread and to prayer. Everyone was filled with awe, and many wonders and miraculous signs were done by the apostles. All the believers were together and had everything in common. Selling their possessions and goods, they gave to anyone as he had need. Every day they continued to meet together in the temple courts. They broke bread in their homes and ate together with glad and sincere hearts, praising God and enjoying the favor of all the people. And the Lord added to their number daily those who were being saved. (Acts 2:42-47)

You cannot have that kind of experience unless you are fully devoted to the cause. The early disciples were sold out to Jesus and to carrying on His teachings through their words and deeds. The early church was not about specialists employing foolproof techniques; it was about sinners receiving grace, committing to change, and living in concert with the wisdom imparted by their faith resources—the Scriptures, the lives of fellow sojourners, and the leading of the Holy Spirit. As a natural result of dedicated discipleship, the church grew exponentially.

Do you know anyone who wants that kind of life? Are you willing to pull out all the stops to help them have it?

Where We're Going

Discipleship is not about reading books and storing up knowledge. My objective, however, is to provide you with information that may help you design a plan for your church and your life that will result in an Acts 2–type of experience. Here's how I hope to accomplish that outcome.

In chapter 2 we will explore some of the nuts and bolts of discipleship—definitions, scriptural justifications, and a framework for the journey.

In chapter 3 I'll present a brief overview of the current state of the church—individually and institutionally—as the context within which we are serving. You cannot intelligently change reality until you understand it.

Chapter 4 will provide an analysis of how we got to our current state of reality. This chapter will help you avoid the same traps and pitfalls that got us to our present condition of ineffectual spirituality.

You cannot get too far without a goal in mind, so chapter 5 will outline the goal of discipleship. Note that this chapter is not a step-by-step plan of action for your church, because every church is unique. But I will offer some adaptable guidelines for the development of your church's agenda.

Chapter 6 will distill for you the findings from my research among a couple of dozen churches across the nation that are doing outstanding work in the area of discipleship. You will discover the philosophies and "best practices" these churches have in common —ideas that are transferable to your church.

> *If we are serious about ministering*
> *to people, we could not have asked*
> *for a better place and time in history to be alive.*

The research led me to see that there are five viable models in place in the highly effective churches we studied.[1] In chapter 7, I will describe those models for you with the expectation that you may want to adapt one of them to your situation.

The final chapter ties it all together and poses one last challenge to your resolve: Are you really committed to being and reproducing committed followers of Jesus Christ?

The new millennium is a tremendous time for us to focus on true discipleship. People are searching for answers, for relationships, for meaning. The church has everything that people are seeking. If we are serious about ministering to people, we could not have asked for a better place and time in history to be alive. The challenges are enormous, of course, but the possibilities for incredible results are equally vast. If we are willing to pay the price to follow the Lord, this is a time of unparalleled potential and promise.

CHAPTER TWO

FOCUS ON THE FUNDAMENTALS

———— ◆◆◆ ————

Jesus is seeking people who are absolutely serious about becoming new creations in Him.

———— ◆◆◆ ————

In the original biblical texts, the term used for *disciple* refers to someone who is a learner or follower who serves as an apprentice under the tutelage of a master. The apostles are great examples of this relationship between a student and master: They followed Jesus, the master teacher and model of the Christian faith, learning from His words and deeds and growing through the practical, hands-on training He facilitated. Discipleship connotes that you are being prepared for a particular lifestyle more than for a specialized occupation.

We might define discipleship as *becoming a complete and competent follower of Jesus Christ.* It is about the intentional training of people who voluntarily submit to the lordship of Christ and who want to become imitators of Him in every thought, word, and deed. On the basis of teaching, training, experiences, relationships, and accountability, a disciple becomes transformed into the likeness of Jesus Christ.

Discipleship, in other words, is about being and reproducing spiritually mature zealots for Christ.

I believe the intensity conveyed by the word *zealot* is important for us to associate with discipleship. Most Christians lack a true understanding of the context within which Jesus' disciples were developed. As a result, we tend to minimize the investment required to be a follower of Jesus Christ. When we hear that the apostles were followers of Jesus, the image that comes to mind is of people who tagged along after the Lord on His walks through the hot, dusty towns of Judea. The followers were there to listen, to watch, and to be amazed at what the Son of God did in their presence.

FOLLOWING JESUS

You and I are "followers" of many different people, organizations, activities, and ideas. For instance, I "follow" the New York Yankees. When they win a game I'm happy for a few seconds, and then I get on with my life. When the Yankees lose a game I'm disappointed for a few seconds, and then I get on with my life. I am not a Yankee zealot—a person who is single-mindedly invested in the day-to-day fortunes of that team.

Contrast that with being a follower of Jesus, especially with what it meant to be in the elite group of twelve. Each of the twelve disciples abandoned his profession. Each lived a minimalist lifestyle, carrying few possessions and having no enduring sense of residential stability. The disciples learned new principles constantly and were expected to apply those principles on demand. Although all they tried to do was help people, they suffered persecution because their Teacher and His ways were so radical and threatening to some of society's powerbrokers. Their training period was for an unspecified duration, but it lasted in excess of two years before being "prematurely" curtailed. There were no textbooks on which they could rely, so they had to be constantly alert and retain all of the information and insights gleaned during their training stage. In short, they had no life apart from what they were being trained to do. Being a follower of Jesus Christ was an all-consuming obsession.

Unfortunately, the twenty-first-century church has many "followers" of Christ in the sense that I follow the Yankees: We dabble in Christianity. That's not what Jesus had in mind when He called us to be His disciples. He is seeking people who are absolutely serious about becoming new creations in Him—individuals who are fanatics, zealots, mesmerized, passionate about the cause, completely devoted to mimicking their model down to the last nuance.

> *The twenty-first-century church has many "followers"*
> *of Christ in the sense that I follow the Yankees.*

Discipleship is not a program. It is not a ministry. It is a lifelong commitment to a lifestyle.

HOW IMPORTANT IS DISCIPLESHIP?

My study of discipleship in America has been eye-opening. Almost every church in our country has some type of discipleship program or set of activities, but stunningly few churches have a church of disciples. Maybe that's because for many Christians today, including Christian leaders, discipleship is not terribly important. If we can get people to attend worship services, pay for the church's buildings and salaries, and muster positive, loving attitudes toward one another and toward the world, we often feel that's good enough. But what does the Bible have to say about the significance of discipleship?

Plenty.

We might start with a brief review of key passages regarding the nature of discipleship. The following are six biblically based insights into the importance of discipleship and corresponding Scripture references for further study.

1. Disciples Must Be Assured of Their Salvation by Grace Alone

Embracing the free gift of salvation made available to us through the death and resurrection of Jesus Christ initiates our journey as a disciple of Christ. Without the relationship made possible by the acceptance of His gift, a person cannot progress as a disciple; rejection of the cross is an insurmountable obstacle to being a committed follower of Jesus. All human beings are invited to become true disciples of the Lord, but to get into the training program, we must confess our sins and accept Christ as our Savior. Until that score is settled, complete devotion to Christ is impossible.

Scriptures regarding salvation and its relationship to discipleship include Luke 13:1-5,22-30; 24:46-47; John 3:16-21; Acts 2:36-39; Romans 3:10-24; Galatians 3:1-5; Ephesians 1:13-14; 2:4-10; Titus 3:4-7.

2. Disciples Must Learn and Understand the Principles of the Christian Life

If we are to truly own and then give away our faith, we must have a deep and complete comprehension of that faith. We live in accordance with what we know; we can give only what we ourselves possess. Therefore, it is imperative that anyone who wishes to be a disciple commit to gaining insight into the nature and substance of the Christian faith and work toward a total integration of the principles of that faith in his or her life. You cannot pass that faith on to others if you are not living it…and you cannot live it if you do not understand it.

The importance of learning and understanding Christianity is exemplified in Matthew 6:33; Luke 14:25-35; Philippians 4:8-9; 2 Timothy 3:16-17; Hebrews 5:11–6:3; James 1:5.

3. Disciples Must Obey God's Laws and Commands

Professing allegiance to a cause is one thing; proving your allegiance through actions that are consistent with the core beliefs and practices of the cause is something else. To be a true disciple does not require perfection, for if it did Christianity would not exist today. True discipleship does, however, demand that an individual constantly strive to live in harmony with God's laws and commands.

It is not enough just to know those admonitions; a disciple is devoted to carrying them out consistently and wholeheartedly. The result is a lifestyle that is distinguishable from the norm: vision, values, goals, relationships, and behavior that are different from the established patterns and accepted norms.

See Luke 10:25-28; Acts 5:29; Galatians 5:16-24; Ephesians 4:20–5:21; Colossians 3:1-17; 1 Thessalonians 4:7; James 1:22-25; 1 John 3:16-24.

4. Disciples Must Represent God in the World

Followers of Jesus Christ are not given the option of telling people, "Do as I say, not as I do." Our lives must reflect the ways of God. But even more than that, we are to be God's ambassadors in the world. We are not called to retreat or to live in isolation, but to be light in the darkness—which requires being in the midst of that darkness. We are to be alert to opportunities to represent God in ways that honor Him. And the Great Commission is clear that we are to pursue the world rather than wait for it to pursue us.

See Matthew 10:16; 28:17-20; Mark 5:18-19; John 17:14-18; Acts 1:8; 2 Corinthians 5:20; Ephesians 4:1; Colossians 1:10; 1 John 2:15-17.

5. Disciples Must Serve Other People

The purpose of discipleship is to help Christians become transformed individuals who imitate Christ daily. Jesus' life was about selfless love of others—a life devoted to serving people. Our objective is to help one another become prepared to understand and address people's needs with the same love, sensitivity, and skill demonstrated by Jesus during His earthly ministry. Discipleship is servanthood; Jesus Himself taught that it is only through serving that one becomes a master.

See Matthew 16:24-28; 20:25-28; Luke 9:1-6; 10:30-37; Acts 6:1-3; Ephesians 2:10; 4:11-12; Philippians 2:1-4; Hebrews 13:16; James 2:14-24.

6. Disciples Must Reproduce Themselves in Christ

The end goal of disciples is both personal and corporate. The personal goal is to live a life worthy of the name *Christian*. The corporate goal is to introduce other people to Jesus, help them to accept Him as their Savior, and enable them to live the life worthy of someone known as a Christian. The Great Commission is not primarily about evangelism, it is about discipleship: "Therefore go and make *disciples* of all nations" (Matthew 28:19, emphasis added). An individual who does not reproduce himself in Christ is not truly a disciple since he does not exhibit the selfless love of the Master.

The command for disciples to reproduce themselves is found in Matthew 28:19. You can also find it in John 15:8. Other relevant passages include Matthew 9:35-38; Acts 4:1-11; 5:42; 13:47.

DISCIPLE MAKING IS NOT OPTIONAL

The viability of the Christian faith, it turns out, is intimately related to engagement in discipleship. Jesus did not spend three years modeling the discipleship process because He wasn't sure how else to end His time on earth. The writers of Scripture did not capture Jesus' words on the meaning of discipleship and the related efforts of the apostles for lack of creative ideas. The apostle Paul did not journey back and forth between the churches he'd started simply to gain frequent-walker miles.

The strength and influence of the church is wholly dependent upon its commitment to true discipleship. Producing transformed lives, and seeing those lives reproduced in others, is a core challenge to believers and to the local church.

LIVING EXAMPLES OF DISCIPLESHIP

Just to make sure we do not miss the significance of discipleship as a lifestyle, the New Testament is crammed with portraits of believers engaged in personal discipleship. The process involves two complementary components: (1) becoming a committed, knowledgeable, practicing follower of Jesus and (2) instilling that same passion and capacity in others. Consider some of the biblical examples provided for us to follow.

Jesus Christ

Jesus began His public ministry by recruiting the twelve men who became known as the disciples. He spent the remainder of His time on earth pouring into them the key lessons required to understand life. His objective was to prepare them to carry on His mission in His (physical) absence. Notice how He approached discipling His followers: teaching, modeling, exhorting, encouraging. We won't do any better than to follow this process.

> *The Great Commission is not primarily*
> *about evangelism, it is about discipleship.*

Paul

Nobody imitated Jesus' model better than Paul did. And Paul's imitation of Christ is incredibly significant because he shows us that it can be done! After being saved and then discipled, he launched into a time of powerful, effective ministry. Paul demonstrates the courage required to boldly represent Christ, the importance of mentoring others, and how indispensable theological knowledge and common sense are in working both inside and outside of the church.

John the Baptist

Although we tend to think of him as a quirky iconoclast, we mustn't lose sight of John's enviable certainty and single-mindedness about his task. Before it was fashionable to be a follower of Jesus—largely because He had not yet emerged as the incarnate Son of God— John was dedicated to pointing people toward God and preparing them for the One who was to come. He was so influential that Herod beheaded him. He was so committed that Jesus went out of His way to be baptized by him. And he was so exemplary that his life story is still told to this day.

THE CHURCH IN JERUSALEM

The first church is described for us in the book of Acts. There may be no better—and certainly no more succinct—picture of a true church than that provided in Acts 2 (note especially verses 42-47). This account is an applied definition of discipleship: the followers of Christ engaged in worshiping, learning, relating, sharing, serving, evangelizing, and praying. The result was numerical growth, cultural influence, and the glorification of God. Their commitment exacted a price—many were persecuted and killed for their faith—but their devotion to Christ resulted in the spread of a dynamic faith that has lasted more than two thousand years regardless of countless political, geographic, sociological, and spiritual roadblocks along the way.

What we see in these examples are people who are committed to both *being* disciples and *producing* disciples of Christ—doing and facilitating. They embrace the principles Jesus taught of obeying God's commands, loving people, expressing gratitude to God through service, strategically training new followers, holding one another accountable, and working in cooperation to achieve the ends of the kingdom. Personal attitudes and behaviors are thereby changed to conform to the dictates of God.

If you want to get excited about discipleship, read the book of Acts. It's hard to read the story of Stephen and not want to jump out of your seat and find someone to mentor. The simplicity and boldness displayed by Peter is inspiring—and given our knowledge of Peter before Pentecost, his story encourages us to believe that we, too, can overcome our deficiencies to serve the Lord with honor and impact. And following Paul on his travels throughout Asia Minor gets you both exhausted and energized. How could one man do so much in such a short period of time?

These are the stories of zealots for Christ! Because we have a glimpse into their lives before they became revered saints, we know that they started off no better than we are. Their stories have become legendary because of their passion for the cause of Christ. Absolutely nothing was more important to them than being disciples of Jesus Christ—and they allowed nothing to stand in the way of fulfilling that glorious opportunity.

THE MARKS OF A DISCIPLE

The marks of a true disciple, then, are simple:

- Disciples experience a changed future through their acceptance of Jesus Christ as Savior and of the Christian faith as their defining philosophy of life.

- Disciples undergo a changed lifestyle that is manifested through Christ-oriented values, goals, perspectives, activities, and relationships.

- Disciples mature into a changed worldview, attributable to a deeper comprehension of the true meaning and impact of Christianity. Truth becomes an entirely God-driven reality to a disciple. Pursuing the truths of God becomes the disciple's lifelong quest.

Take a good look at your life. Are you certain and excited about your eternal destiny as a result of your relationship with Christ? Is your lifestyle one that you could confidently display to God without fear of rebuke? Are you sufficiently conversant in the principles and purposes of your faith that give you meaning, purpose, hope, and parameters?

How about your ministry to others? Do you exploit available opportunities to share your faith in Christ with those who are not believers? Are you committed to assisting any believers in pursuing personal spiritual development?

If you wonder how you're doing as a disciple—and as a disciple maker—let me encourage you to thoughtfully consider ten simple questions:

1. Are you certain that your eternal salvation has been determined by your confession of sins and your acceptance of Christ's gift of forgiveness?

2. Do you consistently obey Jesus' teachings?

3. Do you always love other people in practical ways, especially fellow followers of Christ?

4. Have you put the attractions and distractions of this world in their proper place and focused on knowing, loving, and serving God?

5. Do you carry the burdens of following Jesus with joy?

6. Do you live in such a way as to show others what the Christian life looks like?

7. Do you relate to other Christians consistently, in a spiritual setting and for spiritual purposes?

8. Are you sharing your faith in Christ with those who have not embraced Him as their Savior?

9. Are you helping other believers to grow spiritually?

10. Do you consistently seek guidance from God in all you do?

> *When you are a true disciple of Jesus Christ, you will bear fruit worthy of a follower of the risen Lord.*

The essence of these questions is simple: When you are a true disciple of Jesus Christ, you will bear fruit worthy of a follower of the risen Lord. There is no single test to definitively ascertain whether you are a true disciple, but God has placed His Holy Spirit within you to enable you to discern such things. Questions such as these are mere reminders of the importance of certain types of efforts at growing and serving. None of us would score a perfect ten every moment of every day; we all fall short sometimes. But as Paul instructed us, we must keep our eyes focused on the goal.

It is interesting to notice the divergent characters of Jesus' disciples. Discipleship is about becoming devoted and mature followers of Jesus, but apparently it is not about becoming clones. Christianity does not require us to become bland, uniform, one-dimensional beings. We are able to maintain the idiosyncrasies and unique qualities God bred into us. All God wants to do is transform our hearts from focusing on self and the world to focusing exclusively on Him. Once that transition is underway, He provides ways to use our distinctive qualities for His purposes.

Also note that the disciples who started that global spiritual revolution in Jerusalem were not building the church solely on the basis of accumulated knowledge. We must not forget that discipleship is more than learning the substance of the Bible. Stephen was obviously well schooled in church history and was able to effectively articulate the story of the church, but we also know that, before he was martyred, he was one of the leaders of the outreach to the needy. Paul was one of the world's great debaters, but we also read about his concern for the poor, the widowed, and the sick. Jesus modeled this balance of knowledge and application by dividing His time between teaching and demonstrating love in action—

healing, feeding, consoling, encouraging. Discipleship is an artful blend of what we know and what we do.

BUILDING A DISCIPLING CHURCH

Discipleship cannot occur in a vacuum; it is most effectively accomplished in cooperation with other followers of the Lord. The significance of the local church as a gathering of believers is inescapable: Without the support of a body of like-minded followers, we will not reach our potential as servants of God.

> *Churches that are most effective in discipleship have a philosophy of ministry that places daily spiritual growth at the core of the ministry.*

My studies of thousands of churches across the country have convinced me that discipleship does not happen simply because a church exists. It occurs when there is an intentional and strategic thrust to facilitate spiritual maturity. Specifically, the local church must have a philosophy of ministry that emphasizes the significance of discipleship and promotes a process for facilitating such maturity. The church must provide relational opportunities for congregants, matching those who need to grow with individuals and ministries that facilitate growth. Because serving people is such a crucial dimension of spiritual maturity, churches help people grow by giving them opportunities to meet the needs of others. One of the great—and underutilized—benefits of the church is to provide a means of accountability for those who seek to grow in Christ.

To create a discipling church takes more than having a Sunday school, small groups, or good expository preaching. As we will discuss in a subsequent chapter, churches that are most effective in discipleship have learned what is required among their people: a philosophy of ministry that places daily spiritual growth at the core of the ministry. Programs alone won't get the job done. Knowing what you're striving to produce, having a philosophy that supports that outcome, implementing a plan to accomplish the goal, and evaluating the sufficiency of the outcomes is crucial to successful discipleship. Just as each believer's life is examined to see if it produces fruit, so must each church evaluate its ministry to determine the quantity and quality of the fruit it is producing.

But it all starts with a clear understanding of what we're seeking to produce: people committed to becoming and to reproducing spiritually mature zealots for Christ.

CHAPTER THREE

THE STATE
OF DISCIPLESHIP

———◆◆◆———

Most believers say their faith matters,
but few invest much energy in the
pursuit of spiritual growth.

———◆◆◆———

Discipleship matters.

It matters because Jesus modeled it and commanded it.

It matters because discipleship is necessary for the church to become healthy and productive.

It matters because we cannot reach our potential without spiritual growth.

And it matters because we cannot influence the world unless we can demonstrate faith-based transformation.

How are we doing in the realm of spiritual growth? Are we fulfilling God's expectations of us? Are we avidly striving to fulfill our spiritual potential on earth?

To get a grip on this matter, let's explore a couple of crucial areas. First, let's look at the present attitudes and involvement of born-again Christians in relation to personal spiritual growth.[1] Then let's explore the role currently played by the local church in motivating and supporting believers in their quest for spiritual development.

THE PLACE OF SPIRITUAL GROWTH

Our research discovered an interesting condition. On the one hand, when you ask born-again adults about their goals in life and ask them to rank a series of possibilities, personal spiritual development emerges as one of their top priorities. For instance, four out of five believers said that having a deep, personal commitment to the Christian faith is a top priority for their future. On the other hand, when you ask believers to identify the single most important thing they hope to accomplish in life without suggesting any particular possibilities, only a small minority (20 percent) mentions anything directly related to spiritual outcomes. In other words, most believers say their faith matters, but few are investing much energy in the pursuit of spiritual growth.

How can these seeming contradictions be reconciled? In short, most born-again adults acknowledge that spiritual development is a primary responsibility of a follower of Christ and may be a helpful endeavor, but it is not a pressing need because they believe they have largely mastered the principles and nuances of the Christian faith.

Three of every five adult Christians we surveyed told us they want to have a deep commitment to the Christian faith, but they are not involved in any intentional effort to grow spiritually. They view their challenge as one of spiritual maintenance rather than spiritual development. They contend that because they have embraced Jesus, learned the core lessons from Scripture, and implemented those lessons, all they need to do in the future is continue doing what they're already doing. The one out of five believers who are actively engaged in some type of personal spiritual development activity, besides attending church services, are involved in concerted efforts to learn new insights, live in a more obedient manner, and apply their newfound wisdom in unique and expanding ways.

How do people pursue spiritual development? The most common approaches used by those currently involved in some type of spiritual nurturing process include the following:

- two out of three (68 percent) are involved in a small group or cell group designed to facilitate spiritual growth

- out of four (24 percent) participates in a Sunday school class that motivates them to grow

- one out of every seven (15 percent) is being spiritually mentored by someone

- one out of every nine (11 percent) attends a special class for the purpose of becoming more spiritually mature

The typical individual who allocates some energy to personal spiritual growth spends an average of four hours per week on these endeavors. Most of these people are quite regular in their commitment to spiritual growth: Two-thirds invest time and energy in such matters every week, while more than four out of five growth-oriented believers engage in such activities at least monthly.

WHAT IS "SUCCESSFUL DISCIPLESHIP"?

Our research also points out that most born-again adults are limited in their ability to grow spiritually because they have failed to set any goals for their spiritual development, failed to develop standards against which to measure their growth, or failed to establish procedures for being held accountable for their growth. Only four out of every ten churched believers responded that they had set personal spiritual growth goals for themselves.

Six out of ten believers have no sense of what they want to achieve or become.

Even that figure is inflated, though, since many of the "goals" are not measurable (that is, "to become a better Christian" or "to grow spiritually"), not spiritual (that is, "to be a better person"), or not much of a stretch (that is, "to attend church services"). If we recalculate the statistics on the basis of people's personal spiritual expectations, we find that six out of ten believers have no sense of what they want to achieve or become, and roughly two out of ten have only the vaguest idea of what they might like to achieve or become. That leaves only two out of ten believers who are serious about their spiritual development and have defined rather specific goals.

It is intriguing that when Christians were asked to identify their spiritual goals (see Table 3.1), few believers mentioned more than one goal. For some people that seemed to be a strategic choice—having selected only one goal made it more feasible that

Table 3.1

THE PERSONAL SPIRITUAL GOALS OF BORN-AGAIN ADULTS

(N = 417)

grow spiritually (no specifics)	26 %
live a life that's more pleasing to God (no specifics)	19
be involved in spiritual growth activity (no specifics)	15
read the Bible more, know more Bible content	14
attend church more consistently	13
have a better prayer life	11
serve other people, have a personal ministry	10
participate more frequently in church activities	9
improve the spiritual state of my family	7
have good feelings about myself	2
don't remember the goals	5

(Note: Percentages add to more than 100 percent because people were allowed to provide more than one reply.)

they would satisfy their goal or that they would not become frustrated by having too many unreachable outcomes to achieve. However, for a larger share of the goal-setters, it seemed that the paucity of personal goals reflected the absence of reflection and commitment to growth.

These goals are further challenged by the fact that three out of ten born-again adults admitted that they did not have any plan or process by which they intended to fulfill their spiritual goals. You've probably encountered this before: people who say they have set goals for their development but who have no idea how they will go about making those goals a reality. The result is talk without action, sentiment without substance. (These types of self-deceptions lead some nonbelievers to label Christians "hypocrites.") The unrealistic expectations of believers—that is, if they have good intentions those intentions will somehow come to fruition—often lead them to wander from their faith, feeling as if God has let them down or that they are not capable of spiritual growth.

In fact, when we asked a national sample of believers to describe what they would most like to accomplish in life, both positive and negative signs emerged. The data in Table 3.2 show us that there are some born-again adults who center their lives around their spiritual condition. Unfortunately, those believers are few and far between.

Eight out of every ten believers are more likely to court dimensions of life other than spirituality as the springboard to success and meaning. Elements such as family, career development, and financial achievement are among the emphases most likely to divert people's attention from their spiritual growth. None of these outcomes is necessarily bad or indefensible; however, the infrequent adoption of spiritual maturity as the driving focus of life suggests that to most believers, their faith is a "bonus" or an add-on dimension of their life rather than the priority around which everything in their life revolves.

Table 3.2

WHAT IS THE SINGLE MOST IMPORTANT THING YOU WOULD LIKE TO ACCOMPLISH IN YOUR LIFE?

(base: 450 born-again adults)

being a good parent, raising good kids, having happy kids	29 %
spiritual condition: having faith, going to heaven, doing God's will, evangelizing others, raising my kids to be Christians	20
financial security, comfort, retirement funds, wealth	14
completing/furthering my education	7
making a difference in the world, helping other people	7
experiencing career success, having a good job/career	7
having good health	6
having a good marriage	4
being a good person, being known as a good person	4
having a good life: being happy, being fulfilled	3
nothing in particular	9

(Note: Percentages add to more than 100 percent because some people gave more than one answer.)

Half of the two out of ten who cited some type of spiritual outcome as their crowning achievement in life identified rather basic spiritual realities, such as knowing that they are saved or maintaining faith in God, as their supreme life goal. Is that all we can hope for? Is there no more to the Christian faith than accepting a free ticket to heaven or remaining convinced that God exists? Perhaps this is why half of all born-again adults, and more than two-thirds of born-again teenagers, say they are searching for meaning and purpose in life—in spite of having made a lifelong commitment to Jesus Christ!

The information outlined in Table 3.3 regarding believers' definitions of spiritual success provides another revealing glimpse into the minds and hearts of believers. The good news is that Christians possess a diversity of ideas regarding spiritual success; there is no mindless recitation of one simplistic notion of success embraced by the masses. Clearly, many believers have thought about what makes them successful in God's eyes. Some of the conclusions drawn by the individuals we interviewed evidenced considerable reflection and wisdom.

The disturbing outcomes discernible in Table 3.3, though, are how few Christians seem to possess a "big picture" of spirituality and that very few believers (less than one out of five) describe spiritual success in terms broader than a single aspect of personal maturity. Most born-again adults have a very narrow view of what they are striving to become as Christians, what spiritual maturity might look like in their lives, and what it would take for them to maximize their potential as followers of Christ. The dilemma is not

Table 3.3

WHAT WOULD MAKE YOU SPIRITUALLY SUCCESSFUL?

(base: 417 born-again adults)

following Jesus, patterning my life after His, living as He leads me	15 %
having a personal/growing relationship with Jesus	15
experiencing inner peace/emotional peace	13
being blessed by God	11
having assurance of my salvation, being saved, receiving God's grace	11
believing in God	8
reading the Bible, doing what the Bible says	7
sharing my faith with other people	7
being obedient, behaving appropriately (specific examples given)	6
having a good spiritual life as a family	6
obeying the Ten Commandments, obeying God's rules	5
engaging in appropriate behavior (no specifics)	5
going to church every weekend	4
being an example to others through my lifestyle	4
being happy with life	4
helping other people	3
teaching other people about Jesus, helping others to grow spiritually	2
other (general comments)	20
don't know	14

(Note: Percentages add to more than 100 percent because some people gave more than one answer.)

that believers deny the importance of spiritual growth or have failed to consider the challenges it raises, but that they seem to have settled for a very limited understanding of the Christian faith and their potential in Christ.

OBSTACLES TO MATURITY

Do you get the sense that Christians are honestly trying to grow spiritually, but they're not trying very hard? To verify that intuition, we asked believers about the intensity of their commitment to personal spiritual growth. Not quite 18 percent (one out of every five) said that their effort to grow spiritually is the single most intense commitment in their life today. Half of the believers said that even though they work at spiritual growth consistently, they have not reached the level of maturity or commitment to maturity that they would like. One out of every five said they occasionally delve into spiritual development, but they are not consistent about those efforts. The remaining one out of ten believers admitted they are neither involved nor interested in spiritual development.

> *All of them underscore one problem:*
> *a lack of passion to be godly.*

You can probably guess the reasons why believers are not more zealous about discipleship. Two-thirds told us they were just too busy to give the process the time it requires. One-quarter cited a general lack of interest or motivation to grow. One-tenth said they

HOW SERIOUS ARE BELIEVERS
ABOUT SPIRITUAL GROWTH?

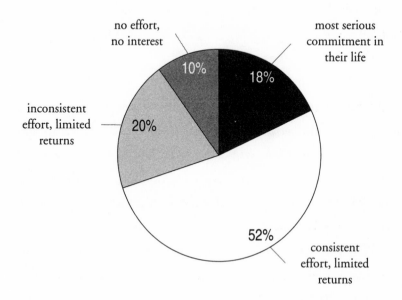

suffered from personal limitations such as emotional or financial problems. One-tenth cited health problems as their barrier.

Does anything strike you about that list of obstacles? Essentially, all of them underscore one problem: a lack of passion to be godly. Such a deficiency raises questions as to how sincere people are about their faith, how real their relationship is with Christ, or how they understand the values of heaven as opposed to those of earth. One thing I have learned about people: If you want something to get done, ask the busiest person associated with your cause. They are busy because they have goals, they prioritize, and they are committed to accomplishing their goals. But what happens within the church? We're all busy when Jesus comes along and asks us to get serious about spiritual growth. What's our response? We may give intellectual assent to the idea, but when push comes to shove, our schedules are already bloated with other, more important tasks, opportunities, and responsibilities. We have passion, but it is not a passion for the matters of God.

Somehow, in spite of having heard the sermons and small-group lessons time and time again, we have missed the point. Can you imagine the early church choosing a different course of action when the problem erupted pertaining to the unfair distribution of food among church widows? Instead of choosing seven disciples to focus on the distribution of food and freeing the other apostles to preach, heal, and evangelize, James might have stood up and said, "Okay, men, that's it. This has gotten too big too fast. Let's get some perspective—things are just out of control. I'm outta here. Who's coming with me? Let's go back to our families, our businesses, and the simple life we knew before this church thing took off."

Or what about Peter, who was jailed in Jerusalem for preaching in public and released at night by the angel of the Lord with the instruction to return to preaching in the public square? It's not likely that Peter, after regaining his freedom, would have taken the fastest horse he could find and galloped that beast as far away as possible from the scene of his persecution, knowing that obedience to the angel's command would have won him further confrontation and hardship.

And I strongly doubt that the apostle Paul ever would have

written a note to Timothy telling his young protégé: *Don't bug me anymore. You're on your own from here on. I've got so many other things to do—cashing in on my international network of contacts, searching for a wife, getting to the Mediterranean for the summer, designing the new line of tents for the fall—I just don't have time for you and all your whining, backbiting congregants. If you have a problem—deal with it!*

Paul endured more than you or I can even dream of because he was a zealous follower of Jesus Christ. If ever anyone had a great excuse to leave the church behind, it was Paul. Consider what he wrote to the believers in Corinth:

> I have worked much harder, been in prison more
> frequently, been flogged more severely, and been
> exposed to death again and again. Five times I
> received from the Jews the forty lashes minus one.
> Three times I was beaten with rods, once I was
> stoned, three times I was shipwrecked, I spent a night
> and day in the open sea, I have been constantly on
> the move. I have been in danger from rivers, in
> danger from bandits, in danger from my own country-
> men, in danger from Gentiles; in danger in the city,
> in danger in the country, in danger at sea; and in
> danger from false brothers. I have labored and toiled
> and have often gone without sleep; I have known
> hunger and thirst and have often gone without food;

I have been cold and naked. Besides everything else,
I face daily the pressure of my concern for all the
churches. (2 Corinthians 11:23-28)

Paul's consistent response to the hardships of following Christ was simple: His lifestyle and ministry reflected the essence of who he was, therefore he would never give up. He would stay committed to obeying his calling and way of life regardless of the earthly circumstances or consequences. When human logic dictated a severe change of course, Paul persevered for one reason: his passion for God. He believed there was no way he could ever outsmart God, outgive Christ, or outmaneuver the Holy Spirit. When you read his story you realize there isn't anything that guy would not have done for his Lord.

THE ROLE OF THE CHURCH

Our research shows that churches have a tremendous opportunity to facilitate deeper commitment among believers. Most born-again adults (95 percent) acknowledge that their church encourages spiritual growth. But only half of the believers we interviewed felt that discipleship is one of the two or three highest ministry priorities of their church; the other half said it is just one of many ministries or programs at their church.

Relatively small numbers of born-again adults reported that their church helps them develop specific paths to follow to foster spiritual growth. Slightly less than half told us that their church had identified any spiritual goals, standards, or expectations for the congregation during the past year. (For many people such goals and expectations were mostly limited to exhortations at the end of sermons to go forth and live in accordance with the points in the sermon. There was no personalization or other, more detailed guidance provided.) Only one out of every five believers stated that their church has some means of facilitating an evaluation of the spiritual maturity or commitment to maturity of congregants. Clearly, the spiritual growth of millions of Christians is being hindered by the lack of detailed assistance and guidance from their churches.

> *Churches have a tremendous opportunity*
> *to facilitate deeper commitment among believers.*

While many Christians were more than a bit cautious about the possibility, nine out of ten said that if their church helped them to identify specific spiritual-growth goals to pursue, they would at least listen to the advice and follow parts, if not all, of it. Very few people (5 percent) said they would flat-out ignore the advice. Only one out of every one hundred believers said they would leave the church if it tried to deliver such an analysis. (Let me emphasize that this relates to congregant-specific advice for spiritual growth, not general, congregation-wide exhortations or pronouncements.)

A majority (55 percent) of the adults who indicated their interest in advice on how to improve their spiritual life also said that if the church matched them with a spiritual mentor or coach, they would be more likely to pursue the changes suggested to them.

Only 7 percent indicated that a mentor or coach would make them less likely to pursue the growth suggestions.

As noted in the previous chapter, discipleship is not a solo adventure; it is interpersonal by its very nature. And, like it or not, people are more likely to grow spiritually when their church is intensely and unswervingly focused on bringing people to maturity in Christ. Such an outcome is not easy to achieve—but it is paramount for the spiritual advancement and health of the individual and of the body of Christ.

Believers are open to a variety of approaches for helping them grow. We asked born-again adults to rate their likelihood of participating in each of eleven different formats of personalized training. The data in Table 3.4 show that of the eleven options, there is no "big winner"—even the most popular option was attractive to only one-third of the believers surveyed. However, there is substantial interest among Christians in doing something that will take them to the next level spiritually. More than four out of five born-again adults chose at least one of the eleven alternatives and said that they would definitely take advantage of that possibility if it were available at their church.

One of the intriguing findings is that the most appealing options were those that are the least intrusive emotionally and personally. For example, the top six options all required very little personal revelation: a devotional guide, a weekly prayer meeting, a self-guided topical study, a group service project, a worship event, and a classroom event. The high-intensity options—such as

Table 3.4

THE SPIRITUAL GROWTH ACTIVITIES IN WHICH BELIEVERS WOULD "DEFINITELY" PARTICIPATE

(N = 465)

using a monthly devotional booklet to guide you through morning devotions	34 %
participating in a weekly prayer meeting with people from your church	26
using an outline of the weekend's sermon for further Bible study on the topic	25
participating in a monthly community service project undertaken by your church	24
attending an additional worship service, either on a weeknight or weekday morning	22
attending a teaching event at your church, one night per week	19
having a weekly meeting with a mentor and three or four other people	18
having an accountability partner to meet with regularly for mutual support	17
participating in a weekly online chat room about Bible principles and applications	14
participating in a class, meeting weekly for one year, on Bible principles	14
enrolling in a seminary-level Bible teaching course, conducted online or via correspondence	12

mentors, accountability partners, and online chats—were farther down the list in their personal appeal. The implication is that many individuals in the church may be scared by the possibility of opening up their lives to others. Building trust is undoubtedly one of the keys to developing a viable discipleship strategy.

COACHING THE SAINTS

One very promising but underutilized tactic for spiritual growth in churches is that of coaching. Coaching, or mentoring, has been quite popular in business and educational circles for the past few years. In fact, half of all born-again adults told us that they had received some mentoring through their church; four out of ten had received mentoring in connection with their job; and three out of ten had benefited from a mentoring process at a school.

Mentoring has influenced the lives of more than forty million adult believers; a majority of all born-again adults claim to have been mentored or coached in something other than sports during their adult life:

- 82 percent—professional or job-related skills

- 68 percent—religious beliefs and Bible knowledge

- 66 percent—how to integrate your faith into your lifestyle

- 65 percent—personal character traits

- 61 percent—relational skills

- 50 percent—parenting skills and perspectives

- 41 percent—personal finances

To some people, mentoring may be a scary proposition. It implies personal openness to evaluation, willingness to consistently work on areas of weakness, and submission to the guidance of someone else. However, an overwhelming proportion of the believers who have been mentored as adults have positive feelings about their experience. Three out of ten said the coaching they received was "life changing." Six out of ten said it had been "very helpful." One out of ten were less enthusiastic, citing it as having been "of some value." Only 1 percent of adult believers who had been mentored said it was not helpful to them.

> *Mentoring has influenced the lives*
> *of more than forty million adult believers.*

Our research revealed another important insight: Past positive experiences in mentoring do not automatically produce believers who are anxious to be mentored in the future. Even though nine out of ten believers assigned high ratings to the value of their past experience when mentored, only one out of every seven adults said they are very interested in being mentored now or in the near future. Another one-quarter were somewhat interested in the possibility.

Why the apparent change of heart? First, most churched adults are busy, and being mentored is a time-consuming, energy-depleting commitment. More people are looking to simplify their lives than are seeking to add more time pressures. Second, participation in coaching requires an admission of incompleteness or immaturity, and people do not lightly admit to such deficiencies. Third, effective coaching requires that the student accept the expertise, motives, and style of the coach—all elements of trust.

The research also highlighted another valuable insight. The types of people most open to being mentored were believers in their twenties, African-American, residents of the West, and upscale individuals. Why these groups? The twenty-somethings typically feel that they lack adequate parenting and that they have been widely rejected by authority figures and older adults. Mentoring represents an opportunity for them to receive the support they feel they were never given. African-Americans generally have a multi-generational, community-based culture in which passing on information, skills, perspectives, and encouragement is part of their heritage. People living in the West are notoriously open to the current fads and trends—of which mentoring is certainly one. Upscale individuals tend to have greater occupational responsibility and challenges than other people, and they are thus open to learning things that will enhance their professional capacity and status. In the business world, mentoring staged a comeback in the United States during the past decade as more and more corporate executives discovered the value of having an expert stand alongside them and help accelerate the speed and depth of their learning curve.

Unfortunately, the bulk of people's interest in being mentored does not relate to spiritual development. The biggest category of interest was religion: 12 percent said they wanted to be coached to grow spiritually, and another 27 percent mentioned wanting to have some type of religious or spiritual mentoring occur.[2] The most popular alternative categories of interest to people included finances (15 percent), job or career development (12 percent), educational achievement (8 percent), parenting (8 percent), self-improvement (7 percent), and relationship building (6 percent).

Would church people entertain the idea of being mentored by someone they trust for the purposes of spiritual development? Yes. Three-quarters of the born-again adults we surveyed said that if

HOW BORN-AGAIN ADULTS WOULD FEEL ABOUT WORKING WITH A MENTOR ON SPIRITUAL DEVELOPMENT

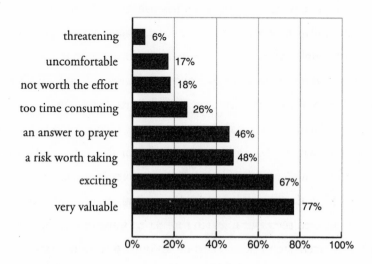

they had that opportunity it would be very valuable; two-thirds claimed it would be exciting. Half of the believers said it would be an answer to prayer. Intriguingly, half also said being mentored spiritually would be a risk but one worth taking. Small numbers said such an activity would be too time consuming (26 percent), not worth the effort (18 percent), uncomfortable (17 percent), and threatening (6 percent).

WHAT DOES IT ALL MEAN?

The chief barrier to effective discipleship is not that people do not have the ability to become spiritually mature, but they lack the passion, perspective, priorities, and perseverance to develop their spiritual lives. Most Christians know that spiritual growth is important, personally beneficial, and expected, but few attend churches that push them to grow or provide the resources necessary to facilitate that growth. Few believers have relationships that hold them accountable for spiritual development. In the end, it boils down to personal priorities. For most of us, regardless of our intellectual assent to the importance of Christian growth, our passions lie elsewhere—and our schedule and energy follow those passions.

Most believers, it turns out, are satisfied to engage in a process without regard for the product. A majority of those who say they are involved in some type of discipleship activity, for instance, contend that because they are involved in a small group, they are on track. Unfortunately, our research shows that most small groups do well with fellowship but falter when it comes to facilitating transformation. Even the teaching delivered in most small groups has little enduring influence in the lives of group participants. Few believers, regardless of the route they select to generate growth, have goals—and most of the goals that have been set are either vague or elementary.

Churches have done a good job of promoting the importance of spiritual maturity, but they have mostly failed to provide an environment in which spiritual growth is a lifestyle. Instead of becoming a natural extension of one's spiritual journey, steady spiritual growth has become the exception to the rule, the domain of the spiritual superstars and fanatics. This is partially attributable to our focus on providing programs rather than relationships that support growth. Although there is openness to the use of spiritual coaching, relatively few people are currently engaged in a mentoring relationship. Our interviews with churches indicate that few churches are intentionally raising up mentors and strategically matching them with congregants.

There is a tremendous need for a more intentional focus on the discipleship process and for the definition of our desired outcomes of such a process. Given the proper motivation, it seems that most believers would be willing to commit to a more demanding regimen of spiritual development.

CHAPTER FOUR

LIVING DIFFERENTLY

———— ◆◆◆ ————

*How well do we measure up
to the example set by Jesus and later
by the disciples in Jerusalem?*

———— ◆◆◆ ————

Jesus was unequivocal about the importance of living differently as a result of faith in Him. The theme of His teaching and modeling was clear:

"Let your light shine before men, that they may see your good deeds and praise your Father in heaven."[1]

His encounter with the rich young man cautioned His followers that being "mostly obedient" doesn't cut it.[2]

He emphasized that the most important commands were to completely love God and other people.[3]

He rejected the acquisition of titles, authority, and worldly honors in favor of humility.[4]

He extolled His followers to be servants who remain oblivious to recognition or compensation.[5]

The Sermon on the Mount was a collection of challenges to

behave in ways that radically departed from the norm but honored God.[6]

His own lifestyle exemplified the ways in which He expects us to live: with passion, zeal, and purity.[7]

His different approach to life was consistently demonstrated through His love and service to those He encountered—from the disciples and the crowds to the woman at the well to Nicodemus the Pharisee—all of whom were initially clueless, yet all of whom were transformed by their interaction with Him.

How well do we, the Christian community in America, measure up to the example set for us by Jesus and later by the disciples in Jerusalem? Let's explore how well we're doing in regard to several pillars of the Christian life as described in Acts and modeled by Jesus in His ministry: worship, evangelism, discipleship, stewardship, service, and fellowship.[8] To be true disciples of Jesus Christ, we need to be growing in each of these dimensions.

WORSHIP

There are two ways to measure our interaction with worship. The simplest and most common way is to evaluate attendance at worship services. The data show that in a typical weekend, about two-thirds of all believers attend worship services at a church. In a given month, about four out of five born-again adults attend worship events. Throughout the year, almost nine out of ten believers attend at least one worship service.

The more challenging evaluation relates to people's experience at worship events. Our studies show that 14 percent of adult believers admit that they have never experienced the presence of God, 14 percent have experienced His presence but not in the past year, and 72 percent have encountered God in a real way within the past year. In a typical worship service, about half claim that they did not experience God's presence or feel that they interacted with Him in a personal way.

Less than one-quarter of all born-again adults consciously strive to make worship part of their lifestyle. For most people, worship implies attending a church service that includes music and preaching.

An underlying issue that must ultimately be resolved is the widespread ignorance among born-again adults regarding the meaning of worship. When we asked people to describe the meaning of worship, 42 percent of all adult believers were unable to provide a substantive or reasonable reply. Among the believers who gave a substantive answer, many gave answers like "attending church" or "listening to the sermon." In total, 58 percent gave us a reasonable response.

> *Less than one-quarter of all born-again adults consciously strive to make worship part of their lifestyle.*

When born-again adults conveyed the most important outcome they want to achieve in this life, less than 1 percent mentioned praising and worshiping God. Few individuals deny the importance of worship, but relatively few understand what it means or have a passion to engage God through worship.

Keep in mind, by the way, that slightly more than four out of every ten adults who attend Protestant church services on a typical weekend are not born-again. Their knowledge of worship—as well

Table 4.1

THE RELIGIOUS PRACTICES OF ADULT BELIEVERS

(N = 882)

In a typical week:	
prayed to God	97 %
had a private quiet time/devotional time	77
attended a worship service	63
read the Bible other than at church	62
attended a Sunday school class	33
volunteered at the church	32
attended a small group/cell group	30
In a typical month:	
read the Bible other than at church	75
donated money to the church	73
In the past year:	
donated money to a church	84
shared faith with a non-Christian	55
In the past two years:	
served as a church leader/teacher	30

as each of the other pillars we are examining—is less advanced than that of the believers who occupy the sanctuary.

EVANGELISM

Slightly more than half of the believers surveyed (55 percent) claimed that during the past year they had shared their faith in Christ with nonbelievers in the hope of seeing some become followers of Jesus. While the research shows that only a small percentage were aware that anyone with whom they had shared had actually chosen to follow Christ, the fact that a majority of believers claims to have engaged in evangelism represents the highest level of involvement we have seen since the early 1990s. What makes the widespread evangelism claims suspect, though, is that the figure contradicts people's attitudes about evangelizing. Less than half of all believers (46 percent) felt strongly that they have a responsibility to communicate their faith to nonbelievers. (This, by the way, represents a significant decline from a decade ago. Millions of born-again adults have been influenced by the cultural cry for tolerance and an acceptance of diversity related to personal beliefs and behaviors.)

No matter what the actual figure of evangelizers may be, most of the faith-sharing believers deserve credit for having shared their faith with non-Christians in spite of feeling that evangelism is not their spiritual gift. Only 1 percent of all adult believers contend that they have the spiritual gift of evangelism.

Most Christians have ample room for development in this

dimension. Indisputably, evangelism is not a priority to most Christians. Less than one out of ten said that they have ever intentionally built a relationship with someone in the hope of being able to lead the person to Christ. Fewer than one of every five believers claimed to know a non-Christian well enough to share their faith with that individual in a context of trust and credibility. And even though a large majority of believers contends that Christians and churches should share their religious beliefs with others, only 4 percent consider sharing their faith with nonbelievers the most important outcome they want to accomplish in their life. This, in turn, is probably related to the fact that only one of every eight adult believers feels adequately prepared to effectively share their faith.

We can add to our perspective on evangelism by listening to the people who represent our local mission field. In surveys we recently conducted among large national samples of unchurched people, we learned that most of them have never been invited to a church by a Christian. Likewise, most unchurched respondents said they had never been told by a Christian what it means to believe in Jesus Christ and never invited to embrace Jesus as their Lord and Savior.

DISCIPLESHIP

In addition to the information communicated in the previous chapter regarding discipleship and spiritual maturity, let's summarize the commitment of believers to knowing God's truths and principles.

Almost all believers own a Bible (99 percent); in fact, more than three-quarters of them own three or more Bibles. Most of them read from the Bible, other than during church services, in a typical week. Three out of four believers indicate that during a typical week they have at least one "quiet time" or private devotional time.

Most Christians take the Bible seriously. One-third believe that the Bible is the actual Word of God and should be interpreted literally. Half perceive it to be the inspired Word of God, completely accurate but containing some symbolism. One-eighth also believe the Bible is God's inspired Word but includes factual and historical errors. The remaining 5 percent contend that the Bible is interesting self-help literature, but not of God.

How Christian Adults View the Bible

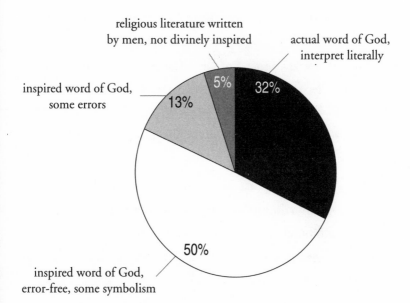

religious literature written
by men, not divinely inspired

actual word of God,
interpret literally

inspired word of God,
some errors

5%

13%

32%

inspired word of God,
error-free, some symbolism

50%

Many believers add to their Bible knowledge through the insights gleaned from public teaching events, such as Sunday school classes, small group meetings, and sermons delivered in worship services. Not quite half of all born-again adults participate in either a small group or a Sunday school class during a typical week.

There is reason to be concerned about what believers claim the Scriptures teach. Take a few minutes to examine the statistics contained in Tables 4.2, 4.3, and 4.4. You will find that while many born-again adults possess biblically accurate perspectives, indefensibly large numbers of believers also maintain views that are nothing short of heretical. At best we can say that most Christians hold theological beliefs that are erratic.

> *There is reason to be concerned*
> *about what believers claim the Scriptures teach.*

When it comes to many of Christianity's many core teachings or central beliefs, millions of believers are sorely deluded in their interpretation of what the Bible says. This situation would be a simple matter of correction if the delusions were limited to just a few aspects of Scripture, such as salvation or righteousness. However, the figures show that huge proportions of Christians—in some cases, even majorities of them—possess views that are exactly the opposite of what the Bible teaches. In summary, here is what adult Christians believe:

Table 4.2

WHAT CHRISTIANS BELIEVE ABOUT GOD, SCRIPTURE, AND POWER

	appropriate reply	percentage
Beliefs About the Bible		
It's totally accurate in all of its teaching	strongly agree	60 %
The Bible teaches that God helps those who help themselves	strongly disagree	20
Beliefs About Deity and the Trinity		
God is the all-knowing, all-powerful, perfect creator of the universe who still rules the world today	strongly agree	92
When He lived on earth, Jesus Christ committed sins	strongly disagree	63
After He was crucified and died, Jesus Christ did not return to life physically	strongly disagree	60
The Holy Spirit is a symbol of God's presence or power but is not a living entity	strongly disagree	38
Beliefs About Spiritual Power		
The universe was originally created by God	strongly agree	95
All of the miracles described in the Bible actually took place	strongly agree	81
Angels exist and influence people's lives	strongly agree	64

Source: Barna Research Group, Ltd. Based on national surveys of 1,000 or more randomly sampled adults 18 or older, conducted July 1999 through July 2000.

Table 4.3

WHAT CHRISTIANS BELIEVE
ABOUT SIN, EVIL, AND SALVATION

	appropriate reply	*percentage*
All people will be judged by God after they die, regardless of their beliefs	strongly agree	90 %
The whole idea of sin is outdated	strongly disagree	86
After death, some people are reincarnated —they return in another life form	strongly disagree	69
There are some crimes or sins people commit that God cannot forgive	strongly disagree	60
All people experience the same outcome after death, regardless of their spiritual beliefs	strongly disagree	56
People who do not consciously accept Jesus Christ as their Savior will be condemned to hell	strongly agree	53
If a person is generally good or does enough good things for others during his or her life, he or she will earn a place in heaven	strongly disagree	49
You have a personal responsibility to tell other people your religious beliefs	strongly agree	46
The devil, or Satan, is not a living being but is a symbol of evil	strongly disagree	43

Source: Barna Research Group, Ltd. Based on national surveys of 1,000 or more randomly sampled adults 18 or older, conducted July 1999 through July 2000.

Table 4.4

WHAT CHRISTIANS BELIEVE ABOUT LIFE

	appropriate reply	*percentage*
It is important to you to experience spiritual growth	strongly agree	86 %
It is more important to please God than to achieve success or acceptance	strongly agree	77
You are certain that God wants you, personally, to help the poor	strongly agree	62
You can lead a full and satisfying life without pursuing spiritual maturity	strongly disagree	56
All religious faiths teach the same basic principles	strongly disagree	53

Source: Barna Research Group, Ltd. Based on national surveys of 1,000 or more randomly sampled adults 18 or older, conducted July 1999 through July 2000.

Three-quarters or more of Christians believe...

- the Bible teaches that "God helps those who help themselves"

- Jesus was born to a virgin

- God is the all-knowing and all-powerful perfect Creator of the universe who still rules the world today

- the universe was created by God

- the miracles in the Bible all happened

- all people will be judged by God

- sin is not an outdated concept

For the most part, these levels of agreement with biblical teaching, while far from perfect, are encouraging. The most distressing item in this list, of course, is the belief that the Bible teaches that "God helps those who help themselves"—the antithesis of biblical truth. As fallen creatures who receive what we have by the grace of God, we are incapable of helping ourselves. It is only our arrogance and self-absorption that causes us to believe that God allows us to determine our reality and that He will simply play along.

Between half and three-quarters of Christians believe...

- the Bible is totally accurate in all that it teaches

- Jesus did not commit sins on earth

- Jesus had a physical resurrection

- the Holy Spirit is not a living entity, just symbolic

- angels exist and influence people's lives

- people are not reincarnated

- people who do not accept Christ as Savior will go to hell

- a person can earn entry into heaven

- Satan is not a living entity, just symbolic

- life is incomplete without spiritual maturity

It is at this level that the belief structure of many believers gets scary. What does it say when one-third doubt the veracity of the Bible? What do we do about the fact that four out of ten believers contend that Jesus committed sins, or that more than one out of four believers rejects the notion of Jesus' having a physical resurrection? How healthy is the church when a majority of believers claim that there is no such entity as the Holy Spirit or Satan? How much progress have we made toward helping people understand God's ways and our place in the universe when a majority says that a good person can earn his or her way into heaven through good deeds?

Between one-quarter and one-half of Christians believe...

- some sins cannot be forgiven by God

- everyone experiences the same outcome after death, regardless of their beliefs

- they have a responsibility to evangelize

- all religious faiths teach the same lessons

What kind of God do one-third of all believers serve who is unable to forgive particular sins? Why believe anything at all if everyone experiences the same outcome after death? Why associate with Christianity if it teaches the same lessons taught by every other faith group?

> *How healthy is the church when a majority*
> *of believers claim that there is no such thing*
> *as the Holy Spirit or Satan?*

To place this in yet a different context, when we asked believers for their views on thirteen of these items, we discovered that only 1 percent of the born-again adults had both a firm and biblically consistent opinion on all thirteen of the statements tested.[9] This is further evidence that believers typically possess a mixture of accurate and inaccurate views on what the Bible teaches.

Waffling About Truth

In addition to these beliefs, we should examine the perspective of believers regarding the most fundamental belief of all: whether absolute moral truth exists. Our country is a nation immersed in moral anarchy largely because Americans have abandoned our historic acceptance of the moral virtues and absolutes emanating from the Bible. These days we are more likely to reject absolute moral truth in favor of relativism, opening the floodgates for a top-to-bottom redefinition of our most important values, attitudes, and behaviors. The rejection of moral absolutes is largely responsible for undermining the health and stability of American society. The shift has occurred largely because believers have fallen asleep at the wheel.[10] Our failure to recognize absolute truth as the cornerstone of a viable worldview and to defend it against the attack of modernism and postmodernism, has resulted in each individual's becoming his own arbiter and standard of truth.

Presently, less than half of all born-again adults (44 percent) are convinced that there is absolute moral truth. The majority of American Christians either believe or yield to the belief that all moral truth is relative to the individual and his or her circumstances. Most believers either hold a weak belief that absolute truth exists (5 percent), that all truth is relative (13 percent), or admit that they don't know what they think about moral absolutes (38 percent). The confusion of Christians regarding truth is verified by other research we have conducted in which we asked about truth in different ways. The outcome was a series of inconsistent views, largely because so few believers have truly grappled with the matter. This incredible confusion about truth is at least partially attributable to the fact that only half of all believers (55 percent) claim that the primary influence on their thinking about moral truth is the Bible or the religious teaching they receive. The other half indicate that family and friends, experiences and observations, emotions and intuition, and other sources provide the greatest influence on their truth perspectives.

CHRISTIANS ARE CONFUSED
ABOUT MORAL TRUTH

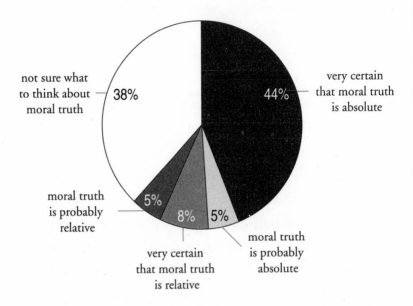

not sure what to think about moral truth — 38%

very certain that moral truth is absolute — 44%

moral truth is probably relative — 5%

very certain that moral truth is relative — 8%

moral truth is probably absolute — 5%

Our waffling on truth has cost us dearly in terms of ministry. In evangelism, millions of believers convey a misleading form of Christianity to nonbelievers, while many others delude themselves into believing evangelism really is not critical because there are various paths to spiritual righteousness. Personal spiritual growth seems less compelling because the need for personal transformation is less imperative; for the most part, we are pleased with the way we are and see a need for minor enhancements at best. Absent certainty about moral absolutes, we are reluctant to "impose" our views of truth and righteousness on others. After all, it's a free society and people believe different things. Of course, without a conviction that God is perfect, omnipotent, and cares about our faithfulness to His commands, worship becomes just another option in our schedule and behavior.

STEWARDSHIP

While we could discuss true stewardship—the management of all of the resources God has entrusted to us on His behalf and for His purposes—let's limit this discussion to how well we manage the financial resources He has provided to us.

In the early church it appears that many of the believers were poor or working class. Today Christians in America have wealth equal to that of the non-Christian segment of the population. The issue is what we do with such a blessing.

> *Believers frequently donate money to their church—*
> *but they don't donate very much.*

Intellectually, we believe that the primary reason God has blessed us is so we may enjoy life and achieve personal fulfillment. Our research has found very few Christians who, without prompting, believe that we have been blessed in order to be a blessing to others.[11]

If we explore what we do with our finances, we find that believers frequently donate money to their church—but they don't donate very much. Three out of four born-again adults give money to their church in a typical month; almost nine of ten contribute to their church during the year. In 1999 the average total donations to churches over the course of the year was just $500.[12] That was two-thirds of all the money the typical believer donated to all churches and nonprofit organizations during the year, but it represents a small fraction of the income of believers.

Most amazing to us was the fact that only 8 percent of all Christians tithed during that year. In fact, twice as many believers (16 percent) gave nothing to their church as gave 10 percent or more of their income.[13]

SERVICE

Christians have opportunities to serve the Lord in many different ways. We know that one-third of them volunteer at their church in a typical week, serving as lay leaders or teachers. Half of all believers volunteer at their church at some time during the year; half do nothing to serve their church or other people throughout the year.

A related issue concerns people's spiritual gifts. Scripture tells us that God entrusts special abilities to His people to accomplish His ends on earth. Every believer is given one or more spiritual gifts for the purpose of serving Him more completely and more capably.[14] Most believers (85 percent) have heard of spiritual gifts. Among those aware of gifts, however, one-quarter do not believe that God has been true to His promise and given them a spiritual gift personally. Among all born-again adults, half either do not know what their spiritual gift is or claim God did not give them a gift, one-quarter mentioned "gifts" that are nowhere to be found in the Bible, and one-quarter listed legitimate gifts they believe they possess.

When it comes to serving the poor, believers are more likely than nonbelievers to devote time and energy to helping the disadvantaged of our society. In the year covered by our survey, 38 percent of born-again adults gave time to help the poor, and 44 percent gave some money to poor people or to organizations helping the poor. Overall, just one of every three born-again adults gave both time and money to helping the poor.

OUR WITNESS TO THE WORLD

In a comprehensive study we conducted in 1997, we compared the beliefs, attitudes, values, and behaviors of believers with those of nonbelievers. After studying 131 different indicators of who we are as people, we concluded that it is difficult for non-Christians to understand Christianity since few born-again individuals model a biblical faith. While there are instances in which believers are different from nonbelievers, when we compare the two groups, the statistical differences are minimal. To the naked eye, the thoughts and deeds (and even many of the religious beliefs) of Christians are virtually indistinguishable from those of nonbelievers. (To give you a perspective on statistical interpretation, realize that a difference of six percentage points is "statistically significant"—but in real terms, that difference is invisible. It is not until you have a twenty-point difference between the two groups that the distinction begins to become noticeable, and not until you have about a forty-point difference that the gap becomes truly challenging to people and influential in their choices.)

Our research enabled us to evaluate the differences between Christians and non-Christians on forty-two variables regarding our nonreligious attitudes and values. Among those forty-two factors, we discovered that on more than half of the items tested (twenty-two) the two groups were statistically identical or quite similar. (These are shown in Table 4.5.) On more than one-third of the items (fifteen) the groups were statistically different but, in practical terms, equivalent (by which I mean less than a twenty-point divergence). (See Table 4.6 to understand these differences.) That leaves five attributes on which Christians are substantially different from non-Christians. Those attributes relate to the acceptability of pornography, profanity, and abortion; the need to "bend the rules" to get by in life; and the rejection of absolute moral truths. (Table 4.7 displays these factors.)[15]

Finally, regarding non-religious behaviors that would be impacted by one's spiritual commitments, we examined fifteen such activities. Of those, nine were statistically identical and six showed statistically significant but pragmatically invisible distinctions. The remaining factor emerged as a visible difference: Christians were notably less likely to drink alcoholic beverages than were non-Christians. (These statistics are displayed in Table 4.8.)

Table 4.5

CHRISTIANS AND NON-CHRISTIANS POSSESS MANY IDENTICAL OR VERY SIMILAR ATTITUDES, OPINIONS, AND VALUES

Indicator	*Christians*	*Non-Christians*
Your family is very important to you	97%	96%
You personally have a responsibility to share what you have with others who are poor or struggling	91	86
The important thing in a relationship is not how much time you spend together but the quality of the time spent together	90	91
You have developed a clear philosophy about life that consistently influences the decisions you make and the way you live	84	81
Your friends are very important to you	81	73
God helps those who help themselves	80	83
One person can really make a difference in the world these days	74	71
There is no such thing as absolute truth; two people could define truth in totally conflicting ways but both could still be correct	67	76
America is a Christian nation	65	66
Nothing can be known for certain except the things you experience in your own life	61	64
Overall, you are very satisfied with your life these days	59	52

Table 4.5 (continued)

CHRISTIANS AND NON-CHRISTIANS POSSESS MANY IDENTICAL OR VERY SIMILAR ATTITUDES, OPINIONS, AND VALUES

Indicator	Christians	Non-Christians
No matter how you feel about money, it is still the main symbol of success in life	51 %	54 %
The death penalty should be mandatory for committing premeditated murder	47	47
You are still trying to figure out the meaning or purpose of your life	36	47
Freedom means being able to do anything you want	35	42
It's almost impossible to be a moral person today	27	33
You favor the idea of doctors who perform an abortion being sentenced to prison for murder	27	20
Whatever is right for your life or works best for you is the only truth you can know	26	35
You can usually tell how successful a person is by examining what he or she owns	19	20
The moral and ethical standards of Americans these days are just as high as ever	17	25
Sometimes it feels like life is not worth living	16	20
It's better to get even than to get mad	12	17

Source: Barna Research Group, Ltd.; 1997 data, national samples.

Table 4.6

On Some Items Christians and Non-Christians Are Statistically Different—But Practically Speaking, the Gap Is Invisible

Indicator	Christians	Non-Christians
You favor allowing students to pray in public schools on a voluntary basis	93 %	74 %
Parents are most responsible for teaching kids about forgiveness	84	71
People are basically good	79	89
When it comes to morals and ethics, or what is right and wrong, there are no absolute standards that apply to everybody in all situations	70	81
The main purpose of life is enjoyment and personal fulfillment	53	66
You favor making it illegal to distribute movies or magazines that contain sexually explicit or pornographic pictures	51	37
When it comes right down to it, your first responsibility is to yourself	41	59
You favor the idea of couples being able to get divorced without going through the courts but by filing notarized papers showing their intent	37	55

Table 4.6 (continued)

ON SOME ITEMS CHRISTIANS AND NON-CHRISTIANS ARE STATISTICALLY DIFFERENT—BUT PRACTICALLY SPEAKING, THE GAP IS INVISIBLE

Indicator	Christians	Non-Christians
The best way for public schools to handle matters related to birth control and sex education among students under the age of 18:		
teach sex education, promote abstinence	36 %	23 %
teach sex education, abstinence as an option	21	20
teach sex education, condoms/birth control available	15	36
leave sex education to parents, no condoms/ birth control	22	15
Before you show someone respect, that person needs to earn it	34	49
Money is very important to you	32	44
Casino gambling should be allowed in all parts of the country	29	42
Even if a person has an incurable disease, a person should not be allowed to end his/her life	27	17
The way things are these days, lying is sometimes necessary	24	40
You favor the idea that homosexual adults should be able to get legally married	23	37

Source: Barna Research Group, Ltd.; 1997 data, national samples.

Table 4.7

CHRISTIANS AND NON-CHRISTIANS NOTICEABLY DIFFER ON SOME ATTITUDES, OPINIONS, AND VALUES

Indicator	Christians	Non-Christians
Abortion is morally wrong	77%	52%
You find it annoying or bothersome to hear profanity on radio programs	75	51
There are moral truths that are unchanging; they are not relative to the circumstances	50	25
To get by in life these days, sometimes you have to bend the rules for your own benefit	35	57
Whether it is acceptable to see pornographic videos or pictures is a matter of taste, not morality	19	42

Source: Barna Research Group, Ltd.; 1997 data, national samples.

WHAT DOES IT ALL MEAN?

Clearly, impeccable historical foundations and the development of good intentions have not been enough to compel believers to lead a life that truly honors and serves Christ. We buy into the importance of worship without really knowing what it means, or we rarely engage in anything beyond rote behaviors. We are generally willing to share our faith, but huge numbers of believers never or rarely do so, and the content of our sharing is frightening. The biblical knowledge of born-again believers is a combination of scriptural substance and worldly wisdom blended into a distasteful

Table 4.8

BELIEVERS AND NONBELIEVERS BEHAVE ALMOST IDENTICALLY

Indicator	Christians	Non-Christians
You consider yourself to be loving	99 %	95 %
You consider yourself to be happy	97	93
You have traditional moral standards	95	86
You consider yourself to be compassionate	94	95
You went out of your way to encourage or compliment someone within the past week for something excellent or special they had done	86	77
You donated money to a nonprofit organization, other than a church, in the past month	47	48
It seems impossible to get ahead because of your financial debt	33	39
You drank an alcoholic beverage in the past month	32	64
You watched an R-rated movie in the past week	30	40
You volunteered to help a nonprofit organization within the past week	29	27
You watched MTV within the past month	26	33
You purchased a lottery ticket in the past week	23	27
You gave money to a homeless/poor person you saw on the street within the past week	13	12
You gambled or placed a bet in the past month	11	22
When a cashier gives you too much change by mistake, you just let it go	10	19

Source: Barna Research Group, Ltd.; 1997 data, national samples.

theological mash. Believers have been incredibly blessed by God with material possessions, but we are loath to return the favor and invest in His priorities. We serve others when we must, but few believers have a love of serving people; our culture has seduced us into loving to be served instead of committing ourselves to meeting the needs of others. We are good at relating to other believers but not very good at having faith-based relationships in which our goal is to help one another mature in Christ. More often than not, our goal is to feel happy, comfortable, and secure—so we surround ourselves with people who share our love for Christ and a willingness to affirm and appreciate us. Most disappointing is a widespread lifestyle among Christians that fails to demonstrate the practical realities of the Christian faith.

Is there room for improvement in the area of discipleship? You bet.

HOW WE GOT HERE— AND WHERE WE GO FROM HERE

———◆◆◆———

*Why we've been ineffective as disciple makers
—and why there's reason for hope.*

———◆◆◆———

When discussing the findings of the previous chapter with church leaders from across the country, I receive three common reactions.

The first reaction is to deny the facts. "I don't know who you talked to, but I know those figures can't be right. It's certainly not an accurate description of the people in my church. I know my people. They think and act differently than that," is a typical response from pastors.

When I ask how they know that their people are different from the national norms, the reply is also rather consistent: "I just know. I talk to them and they tell me things that are very different than what your numbers describe. Our church has been blessed with people who are more spiritually mature than most, partly because we do a good job of building them up in Christ."

In other words, these pastors have no objective measure of the alleged difference between their people and the Christian masses. They believe their people are different based on assumptions, intuition, and anecdotal evidence (personal stories).

The second common reaction is to feel discouraged. "Man, that's depressing. I almost feel like it's not worth continuing in ministry. After giving it our best shot, if that's the best we can produce, then why bother?" Again there are assumptions underlying this viewpoint: We have done our best; the current state of affairs is the best we can hope for; and there are no alternative strategies that might improve the product of our efforts.

The third common response is for church leaders to appreciate and absorb the information because it clarifies the nature of the challenges and opportunities facing them. "Well, we certainly have our work cut out for us, don't we?" said one pastor I interviewed. "But it sure helps to know where we're falling short so we can respond more appropriately to people's needs. Just look at the need and suffering out there! What a great time to be in ministry. If you can't make a difference in the midst of this situation, you probably can't make a difference anywhere!"

In other words, rather than reject the findings as aberrant, these leaders accept the findings as insightful and motivating. They do not get hung up on the personal implications of the outcomes ("This means I'm a failure") or the magnitude of the challenge ("This is too big a job for us to tackle"). Instead, these leaders see the statistics as a progress report on an unfinished work ("It looks like we need to emphasize that aspect of ministry instead of this one").

> *You are among the leaders whom*
> *God has raised up for a time such as this.*

As you reflect on the information presented in chapters 3 and 4, what is your gut reaction? You might be inclined to reject the findings outright. However, if you choose to view the statistics as strategic wisdom that can make you a more effective servant of Christ, then you probably are going to be one of the church leaders who will bless heaven, the church, and our society with irrefutable evidence that God is at work in the lives of His people. You are among the leaders whom God has raised up for a time such as this—a confusing, challenging, daunting era in which His people have a unique capacity to help restore our world to moral and spiritual sanity. If you remain focused and strategic in your ministry, you are likely to see dramatic results in people's lives as they struggle to grow in their faith.

How We Got to Where We Are

One hallmark of effective church leaders is that they not only refuse to accept defeat, but they also strive to improve whatever they are doing. They love statistics and other objective evaluations of their situation because those indicators allow them to pinpoint what does and does not work and to fine-tune their efforts and enhance their efficacy. They do not take personal offense at reports that suggest some of their efforts have failed to produce the desired results; they thrive on such reports because the information enables them to refocus their efforts and avoid wasting resources on unproductive activities.

As we evaluate the current condition of discipleship in the American church—again, defined as activity that guides individuals to become spiritually mature zealots for Christ who then reproduce equally passionate and mature followers of Christ—we must take inventory and change those practices and perspectives that are obstacles to the desired outcome. What ideas and practices have caused us to lose sight of the biblical goals of authentic worship, passionate commitment to spiritual development, sensitive-yet-strategic evangelism, consistent servanthood, loving and challenging relationships, and holistic stewardship?

Nine reasons have emerged from my research as to why we have struggled so mightily in the midst of an environment of unprecedented opportunity. In all likelihood, one or more of these barriers explains some of the difficulty you may be encountering in your ministry.

1. Few Churches or Christians Have a Clear, Measurable Definition of "Spiritual Success"

The old adage warns us, "If you don't know where you're going, any road will take you there." That's an indictment of contemporary Christian discipleship. We have assumed that if a church provides consistent events, biblical information, and appealing programs for people, and the people consume those offerings, then the users will grow. But we rarely stop to figure out in practical terms what God expects of us, to assess how we measure up to those expectations, or to determine what we must do to improve our performance with respect to those desired outcomes.

Lacking a clear notion of what we're trying to become as believers, we often settle for something less than the biblical standard—and certainly less than what we are capable of becoming. Why? If success is negotiable, why not include "comfortable and easily achievable growth" among the factors that make us successful?

How instructive it is to discover that when pressed to do so, not only have most Christians and church leaders failed to specify what "spiritual success" means, but they do not feel compelled to work out a definition of such an end point or destination. The result is that believers and churches have embraced a cheap facsimile of spiritual success without remorse—or in many cases, without the realization that they have "dumbed down" Christianity.

2. We Have Defined "Discipleship" as Head Knowledge Rather Than Complete Transformation

Talk to church leaders about their discipleship strategies and you usually hear about teaching events and programs. Sunday school, small groups, Christian education classes, seminary courses, study groups, reading groups, video curriculum, Vacation Bible School —we have countless ways to communicate empirical information based on Scripture. All are laudable and certainly needed. But it is inadequate to simply fill people's heads with Bible verses and principles. If you doubt that, please reread the Synoptic Gospels and underline Jesus' words to the Pharisees and Sadducees during each encounter He had with them. The religious leaders of Jesus' time had memorized more Scripture and religious content than most of us can imagine. Yet they were Jesus' models of how not to live. Why? Because they were "all head and no heart." They knew the data but ignored its application.

Perhaps more leaders than we know continue to follow the approach of Martin Luther, who disdained the book of James in the New Testament. Some accounts suggest that Luther wished it had not been included in the canon of Scripture. But that letter to the leaders of the early church is incredibly significant because it pounds away at one consistent message: Faith that is not wholly integrated and consistently lived out is a charade. The issue is not that we must choose which element to esteem over the other—that is, siding with either Bible knowledge or a righteous lifestyle—but that each must support the other.

> *Faith that is not wholly integrated*
> *and consistently lived out is a charade.*

The statistics in the preceding chapters underscore our need for both biblical knowledge and the application of that knowledge in practical ways. Becoming spiritually mature in our imitation of Christ demands that we give both the head and the heart sufficient opportunity to grow and to make a difference in our lives and in the world.

3. We Have Chosen to Teach People in Random
Rather Than Systematic Ways

As we survey the practices of churches, we find that most churches are content to provide their people with biblical substance. The problem is not that the content itself is weak, but that the content is not provided in a purposeful, systematic manner. As a result, believers are exposed to good information without context and thus lose that information because they have no way of making sense of it within the bigger picture of faith and life. Consequently, we rate sermons on the basis of their value to what we're experiencing at the moment and assess the usefulness of books and lessons in terms of how entertaining or erudite they are. Ultimately, believers become well versed in knowing characters, stories, ideas, and verses from the Bible, but they remain clueless as to their importance.

Think of the way we teach people about Christianity as a massive game of "Connect the Dots." In our version of the game, we do not put numbers next to the dots, which renders players incapable of connecting the dots in the fashion intended. All of the dots are provided and are pictured in exactly the right place, but if we don't provide players with a sense of direction or the big picture, failure is inevitable.

We have found that few churches intentionally guide their people through a strategic learning and developmental process that has been customized for the student. We push everyone through the same generic journey, expecting all to "get it" at the same time and in the same way as they simultaneously develop into mature believers. Effective discipleship doesn't work that way. Until we assume a more strategic approach to delivering insights and outcomes within a viable mental and experiential framework, we will continue to be frustrated by the results of our well-intentioned but poorly conceptualized efforts to grow disciples.

4. There Is Virtually No Accountability for What We Say, Think, Do, or Believe

True growth demands accountability. However, few churches have systems by which they measure what is happening in the lives of their people. Few believers have lined up a trustworthy and competent partner who will hold them accountable to specific and measurable goals. The result is that we operate on the basis of feelings, assumptions, and hopes rather than tangible, measurable realities.

Small groups may provide an environment within which accountability may occur, but our studies show that such accountability is superficial and uncommon. We tend to be most focused upon evaluating people's knowledge; there are only limited attempts to hold people accountable to grow beyond information acquisition and retention.

5. When It Comes to Discipleship, We Promote Programs Rather Than People

How many churches have a dynamic database or some other means of consistently and objectively tracking the spiritual development of individuals in the church? Very few. How many churches have created a successful mentoring or coaching program? Again, very few.

A discipleship-oriented database implies both a commitment to staying in touch with people's growth and a desire to consistently improve the spiritual condition of the individuals within the church. Few churches have a life-changing mentoring or coaching program because such a process demands extensive knowledge of the qualities and capacities of the coach and the student as well as the ability to wisely pair mentors with appropriate protégés. These are people-intensive processes. Most churches are not structured or emotionally geared to master such processes.

> *Growing true disciples is not about maintaining tight control.*

Even though churches claim that they are devoted to developing people, the most effective developmental procedures known to us today are generally ignored in favor of standardized programs such as Sunday schools and small groups. Please don't misunderstand—such programs have a useful place within a church. However, we should recognize that in addition to their positive developmental features, classes and groups are often embraced as a way to organize large groups of people into an orderly process that can be easily managed and controlled. If we're honest with ourselves, we will have to admit that the absence of real measures of personal growth testifies to our concern about style over substance and to our commitment to action instead of impact.

Growing true disciples is not about maintaining tight control. It is about letting go to see what God, through His Holy Spirit, can do in the life of a believer who truly wants to mature in Christ. Just as Jesus accomplished the maturing of His followers through a personal relationship focused on creating a particular kind of person, so should we be wary of becoming too structured and programmatic.

6. The Primary Method on Which Churches Rely for Spiritual Development—Small Groups—Typically Fails to Provide Comprehensive Spiritual Nurture

The problem is not the approach. Having small groups of people committed to helping one another grow can be incredibly effective. There is ample evidence of this in the Bible and in various churches across the nation. But we don't see greater life transformation through small groups because we have not paid attention to the capabilities of the group leaders and teachers, and the substance that gets shared in the group settings is often plagued by superficiality, misrepresentation, or the absence of application. Too many resources are spent recruiting people for groups and too few resources in preparing people to develop within the groups.

7. Church Leaders Are Not Zealous About the Spiritual Development of People

In our interviews with senior pastors of Protestant churches across the nation we discovered that, while they give verbal support to the idea of spiritual growth, they often are not personally devoted to strenuously advocating spiritual transformation. This deficiency is witnessed in several ways.

First, few congregants describe their pastor as a role model or as a zealot for Christ. While it is unhealthy to place the pastor on a pedestal as the paragon of Christianity, it is even more dangerous for the people not to have appropriate pride in the character and commitments of their spiritual leader. If nothing else, congregants ought to feel that they would be better people if they were to follow the spiritual example set by their pastor. We find, however, that most believers have no clue what the spiritual life of their pastor is like and therefore have little impetus to emulate that leader.

Second, surprisingly few pastors make discipleship a top priority within their ministry. They may incorporate discipleship into the church's agenda and ensure that some funding and warm bodies are allocated to the process, but they do not throw the full weight of their influence behind the significance of becoming spiritually mature. Prioritizing the church's ministries is one of the tough juggling acts pastors perform. Every step along the way, advocates of one ministry or another—all of which are good, necessary, beneficial ministry ventures—are lobbying for the pastor's public support. But ultimately that's what makes a great leader: the ability to juggle all of the possibilities successfully while focusing the greatest quantity of resources on the most productive activities. To some extent the Christian church lacks real disciples because our spiritual leaders have inadequately prioritized that outcome.

Third, when pastors describe "success" for their church, attendance, revenue, programs, and square footage frequently constitute the practical dimensions of success. Surprisingly few pastors indicate that success relates to the spiritual quality of the lives of their

. More often than not, you hear about the quantity of
icipating in a group event or activity.

ie that pastors do not have the professional weight or
public standing they once did in America. However, among people
within the church, the pastor is still a person of influence. One
application of that influence relates to setting the church's ministry
agenda. When senior pastors downplay discipleship, the message
comes through loud and clear: "It's helpful, but optional."

8. We Invest Our Resources in Adults Rather Than in Children

In all aspects of life, people tend to do that which is most comfortable and natural for them. Perhaps that explains why we invest
so much of the church's money in ministering to adults. If we were
to objectively assess where we will get the greatest return on this
investment, we would instead pour our resources into ministries to
children. The work we have done in studying evangelism and discipleship has shown that once children reach the age of twelve or
so, the chances of changing how they think and behave are limited.
The chances of changing adults are very slim.

Does this insinuate that God cannot completely reform an
individual, regardless of his or her age? No. Does it imply that I
believe the Bible is wrong when it says that believers become
regenerated beings after they encounter Christ? No. It is a simple
recognition of human reality. Old habits are difficult to break.
Established patterns of thought and behavior die hard. People can
certainly change no matter how young or old they are, but positive
change is so much easier and permeates much more deeply when

people are young. When we focus more energy on resuscitating adults rather than nurturing children, we have more ground to cover because we have to undo much more than we would in working with children.

As Solomon once wrote with great wisdom, "Train a child in the way he should go, and when he is old he will not turn from it."[1]

9. We Divert Our Best Leaders to Ministries Other Than Discipleship

A leader casts a compelling vision of a preferable future for people to embrace. It is that persuasive mental picture of a better self and better world that is used to motivate people to action. When you have an individual with good skills but little, if any, leadership ability, discipleship fails to get the motivational push it needs.

Congregants are busy. They are trying to make ends meet, keep their marriages and families together, maintain the house and yard, get ahead in their careers, stay abreast of world events, stay physically fit, stay in touch with their friends and extended families, and invest their retirement funds wisely. In the midst of all of this, the church urges them to get involved in discipleship. "Why?" they ask. "I attend church pretty regularly, enroll the kids in Sunday school and VBS, put my hard-earned money in the offering basket each week, pray before meals and whenever else I get a spare moment, and try to read the Bible whenever the opportunity presents itself. How much more am I supposed to do for the church? It's just never enough!"

Without a true leader at the helm of the discipleship function, you almost cannot fault believers for missing the point. A good leader can make the commitment to spiritual growth seem not like a chore but a privilege; less like a command from God (though it is) and more of a glorious opportunity to join an elite group.

Good leaders motivate, mobilize, direct, and resource people to fulfill a vision. Too often we present the options for personal growth and assume our people will be quick to embrace the possibilities and benefits. When they don't climb aboard, we shake our heads and bemoan their lack of commitment—without realizing that they indeed are committed, but mostly to those things that fit within their vision of a meaningful life. Our failure to place competent leaders in the disciple-making process of the church has enabled the people to completely misunderstand the opportunity we are presenting to them.

WHERE DO WE GO FROM HERE?

So where are we trying to go with discipleship? What are the specific outcomes that we are striving to achieve, and what type of process will facilitate those results? Here is my take on our objectives.

1. Passion

The true disciple of Jesus Christ is someone who is completely sold out to Christianity. To determine whether you really are a disciple, the relevant question concerns your level of commitment: *To what are you absolutely, fanatically devoted?* Jesus did not minister, die, and rise from the dead merely to enlist fans. He gave everything He had to create a community of uncompromising zealots—raving, unequivocal, undeterable, no-holds-barred spiritual revolutionaries. He has no room for lukewarm followers.[2] He is not interested in those who have titles, prestige, and self-sufficiency. He is searching for the broken, hopeless, helpless, spiritually dependent individuals who readily acknowledge that they cannot make any headway without a total and absolute dependence upon Him. He is seeking the hearts of those who are willing to surrender everything for the blessed privilege of suffering for Him, just as He suffered for us. He wants people who are dedicated to getting beyond the offer of mere salvation to those who are willing to do what it takes to complete a personal transformation.

> *To what are you absolutely, fanatically devoted?*

Discipleship is a lifelong calling that demands every resource we will ever muster.

Discipleship is about passion to reach our full potential in Jesus Christ.

2. Maturity in the Fundamentals of Ministry

As we saw in chapter 4, there are a small number of ministry components to which we must be dedicated. Those include worship, evangelism, discipleship, servanthood, stewardship, and Christian fellowship. In other words, we are to dive into a process that will facilitate personal spiritual formation and mold us into the likeness of our ultimate role model, Jesus Christ. Our discipleship, or personal spiritual growth, efforts should be designed to develop us in these six primary areas. There are many related activities, of course—prayer, confession, etc.—but our energies should be geared to strategically improving ourselves in these core dimensions.

3. A Biblical Worldview

If you are to act like a Christian, you must think like a Christian. And to think like a Christian, you must be fully immersed in the knowledge of your faith and the application of its principles in godly practices. Because every thought, word, and deed has consequences, every choice we make must be carefully considered. The only way to truly ensure that we represent Christ well in every aspect of our lives is to respond to reality on the basis of a Bible-based worldview. In other words, we must filter every choice through a mind and heart so saturated with God's perspectives that our choices reflect His choices. Our fallen nature prevents us from flawlessly representing the ways of God, but the more we own His truths and principles, the better we will be at living a truly Christian life.

4. Standards and Accountability that Foster Spiritual Growth

Human nature distorts our perspective. Rather than set our sights on the ultimate prize and sacrifice whatever it takes to reach that goal, we usually slither down the path of least resistance and get by as simply as possible. Christian discipleship deems such behavior a failure. We serve a perfect, holy, omnipotent God who yearns for us to imitate His Son. To settle for anything less than our absolute best is disrespectful and indefensible.

However, because we live in a world that accepts second best and halfhearted efforts, we often set our sights lower than we should. Only through adhering to a tireless process of accountability, in which we are motivated and pushed to reach high standards, will we rise to the heights God intends for us to reach. Left to our own devices, we can fool ourselves into believing that we have done better than before—perhaps even the best we can hope to achieve—when in fact we have barely nudged ourselves forward. Reliance upon a community of loving and supportive but high-minded peers in Christ is necessary if we are to make true progress in our spiritual development.

What's Barna Been Smokin'?

Not long ago I had a conversation with the pastor of a large church. We have become friendly enough that we can shred each other's best ideas and analyses without offending or emotionally crippling each other. I ran the above ideas past him.

He laughed, caught his breath, stared at me seriously for a few moments, then burst out laughing some more. Once he regained his composure, he drilled into me. "Barna, what have you been smokin', man? Pass me that pipe, brother, because I want to leave reality and experience your plane of existence. Are you nuts? I dare you to name me one church—*just one*—anywhere in this entire nation of ours that does what you just described. You armchair theoreticians make me nauseous. You're probably going to write this wacko idea in a book and make thousands of pastors suffer guilt because they haven't reached this mythical nirvana you're proposing as a standard. Go ahead, name me one church that does these things."

Our debate raised some wonderful—and for me, deeply disturbing—questions. Is it expecting too much to desire such genuine life transformation in twenty-first-century America? In a world where people are ruled by their calendars and the rule of the calendar is "No more—all full," is it reasonable to expect people to make spiritual growth a top priority? In an age where the pace of life sucks the energy out of us, is it feasible that people could be passionate about something as seemingly intangible as faith? In a world in which relativism and tolerance reign, are we just fooling ourselves to imagine that Christians might be willing to depart from the norm and voluntarily submit themselves to honest scrutiny and accountability by peers? In a nation where we're fortunate to get people to remember that the Old Testament precedes the New Testament in the Bible, is it possible for Christians to adopt a biblical worldview that truly changes the way they think and behave every moment of every day? Is there a church anywhere that really accomplishes these things?

To God's glory—and my relief—it's now my turn to laugh.

My friend's laughter rang in my ears for months. In fact, I seriously questioned whether to continue researching this topic. My friend's ongoing harassment regarding the obstacles of creating such a faith community took a toll on my mind. In all honesty, my desire to complete the research project on discipleship became nothing more noble than a desire to finish what I had started—and to get some benefit from the huge research investment our company had made. I decided that we would carry out the final step in the two-year process: beating the bushes throughout America to find and study churches that carry on effective, life-changing discipleship ministries.

To God's glory—and my relief—it's now my turn to laugh. In the next two chapters I'll describe for you the inner workings of two dozen churches that are doing the very things my friend had deemed impossible. Chapter 6 will reveal many of the common characteristics these churches possess and that you, too, can embrace in your ministry—regardless of your church's size, theological leanings, or target audience. In chapter 7, I'll share five specific models through which these stellar churches accomplish such audacious ends.

BHAGs AND WOWs

The results achieved by these churches are what business guru James Collins would call a "BHAG" (Big, Hairy, Audacious Goal) or bestselling author Tom Peters would call a "WOW!" (as in "this is *incredible*—where do I sign up?").[3] If you felt weighed down by the depressing statistics and descriptions in chapter 4, please don't despair. The next two chapters should lift your spirits and stimulate your mind and heart. If you're like other Christian leaders with whom I've shared these models, you'll find fresh motivation to develop a discipleship process that wins hearty shouts of "I *love* Jesus! I *love* this church! I *love* being a Christian!" from your congregants.

We have made mistakes in the church. We have failed our Lord and we have failed His people. It's time to get it right. So let's learn from our pioneering colleagues who have blazed the trail for us.

CHAPTER SIX

THE KEYS TO HIGHLY EFFECTIVE DISCIPLESHIP

What two dozen successful churches can teach us about growing true disciples.

Let me tell you how various churches across the nation are producing true disciples of Jesus Christ.

We had the privilege of studying two dozen churches in depth to determine what makes their ministries so effective. We discovered that, when it comes to disciple making, they share some common perspectives and practices. We also found that there seem to be five distinctive models by which these churches facilitate genuine followers of Christ. In this chapter I want to describe the perspectives and "best practices" of the churches that are producing great disciples. In the next chapter I'll share the core components of the five models.

What makes me claim that these churches are doing a great job?

First, they are regarded by other ministry professionals as experts in the arena of discipleship. In most cases we learned of these churches from the recommendations of people who have experience working with or studying hundreds of churches.

But we know very well that appearances can be deceiving and that outsiders sometimes misjudge the true state of affairs at a church. So our second requirement was that we conduct extensive interviews with the leaders of these churches and ask probing questions to get at what really happens. Interestingly, more than half of the churches originally recommended to us as being highly effective at disciple making were eliminated once we completed this level of interviews.

Finally, in most cases, one or more of our staff spent some time (usually incognito) experiencing and observing what actually happens at the church. The result was a rather well-rounded examination of the spiritual development process at these churches. The bottom line was that we had firsthand evidence that people's lives were being consistently transformed so that they became more Christlike. Effective discipleship is about life transformation, and these were churches that facilitated such life change.

UNLIKELY TO STAY SMALL

The size of the churches we studied most closely ranged from 150 to about 4,500 adults who attended the church on a typical weekend. The churches in our sample that had the fewest people (approximately 150 adults) are probably not of that size anymore.

By the time you read this they will likely have eclipsed the 200 mark and will be inexorably headed toward 300 and beyond.

> *We quickly learned that a church engaged*
> *in effective discipleship is a church*
> *that will grow steadily and solidly.*

I had hoped to find a wealth of great discipling churches in the 100- to 400-adult range, but we quickly learned that a church engaged in effective discipleship is a church that will grow steadily and solidly. Why? Because people love to be cared for, and a church that emphasizes genuine spiritual care and facilitates real spiritual growth will be a magnet. This is like a parent-child relationship. A loving parent disciplines the child. The child overtly complains about the discipline but covertly cherishes that shaping influence, recognizing that it reflects the parent's love and is in the child's best long-term interests. Christians are the same way. We may complain about all the effort it takes to become or build a true disciple, but the more people sense that the church's regimen is not just busy-work but is truly developmental, the more committed they become to the process and the more other people are attracted to that church.

By the way, the highly effective disciple-making churches we studied come from a wide variety of theological positions (both sides of the Calvinist-Wesleyan divide), geographic locations (all four regions of the United States), and ages (churches ranging from 7 years old to more than 150 years old).

THE BASELINE DEFINITIONS

When we asked the church leaders to describe what discipleship means to them, no two churches gave exactly the same definition. However, we found that there were nine components that their definitions had in common.

1. *Passion.* Each church understood that discipleship without passion is merely organizational programming. Several churches arrived at the importance of passion by having spent years struggling to develop a process that worked—and learning that until the people are passionate about becoming Christlike, no amount of great teaching or cutting-edge techniques will get you where you need to go.

2. *Depth.* The ultimate objective is to enable people to plumb the depths of the Christian faith and truly "own" it. Extensive knowledge about Christianity is insufficient. Extensive ministry activity is, in itself, insufficient. Personal growth without spiritual reproduction is indefensible. These churches are committed to fostering the development of totally Christian believers.

3. *Maturity.* The end product is for the person to reach his or her highest earthly potential in Christ. Thus total personal commitment to becoming spiritually mature is one of the early indicators of success in the process.

4. *Practice.* The emphasis is not on knowing what it means to be a mature Christian or knowing how to become spiritually mature. Rather, highly effective disciple-making churches emphasize *being* spiritually mature— that is, knowing, doing, and being all that Christ has called us to be.

5. *Process.* Discipleship is not a destination but a journey. We will never achieve complete spiritual maturity this side of heaven. We may, however, enjoy the journey, note progress, and continue to grow as we pursue spiritual completeness.

6. *Interactive.* Discipleship must be done in community rather than in isolation. Other people provide a level of objectivity, accountability, creativity, and encouragement that we cannot muster by ourselves.

7. *Multifaceted.* The disciple-making process incorporates a variety of thrusts toward building us up in Christ. Just as the church is to encompass several specific ministry thrusts, so should each disciple grow in various areas of spiritual maturity.

8. *Lifelong.* It is not possible in this life to complete the process of becoming spiritually mature. Therefore, we must be involved in discipleship for the long term,

engaged in a permanent process of shaping and being shaped, of struggling and mastering.

9.   *Christlike.* The model of our efforts is Jesus Christ. When we lose a sense of how we're doing, what we're striving to achieve or what else we must incorporate into the process, the definitive marker is the Lord Himself. All other models are mere imitations; our true point of comparison is Jesus.

"SUCCESSFUL DISCIPLESHIP"

While each church we studied had its own way of communicating what "successful discipleship" means, the nature of their descriptions was similar. Some churches discussed specific ministry outcomes related to worship, evangelism, service, and knowledge. Others talked about more general measures, such as personal empowerment, consistent growth, exploitation of spiritual gifts, or a deepening relationship with Jesus Christ. A few churches identified Bible passages such as Galatians 5:22-24 (the fruit of the Spirit) or 1 Timothy 3 (character qualities) as the substance they refer to when assessing their progress.

MEASURING PROGRESS

When it comes to evaluating how well people are doing in their efforts to emulate Christ, the truly effective churches go beyond collecting and reciting affirming anecdotes. Each of these churches uses specific tools—most developed in-house—to provide a sense of what is happening spiritually in people's lives. These tools include knowledge measurements, behavioral assessments, gift inventories, attitudinal and behavioral surveys, and goal statements and measurements. No church argues that these inventories provide a completely accurate picture of reality; instead, they view their tools as flawed but objective—relatively consistent instruments that aided in determining whether progress was being made from year to year.

> *"If all I have to rely on is my people's say-so*
> *about their growth, I'm in trouble."*

The purpose of the tools was not to claim with certainty that a specific percentage of the congregation knew a given principle or behaved in a particular way, but to indicate that, compared to a year before or in relation to goals that had been set by congregants, the church was at a given level of achievement.

I was impressed by the sensitivity the churches' leaders displayed regarding the frailty of their instruments—and by their commitment to using some tangible, objective yardsticks of progress. "If all I have to rely on is my people's say-so about their growth, I'm in trouble. It's just human nature for us to overestimate our own progress," explained one of the pastors. "I need something that takes the measurement process out of my hands so I'm not the bad guy—something to show me what I need to ask people about so I can hold them accountable to the standards and objectives we've agreed upon."

The measures used by the churches are not limited to personal-growth assessments carried out by individuals. Most churches also employ other general measures of health and well-being, such as:

- the number of volunteers

- how easy or difficult it is to recruit people for ministry responsibilities (for example, Sunday school teachers, feeding the homeless, maintaining the church buildings)

- the number of people who turn in a personal growth plan

- the number of visitors attending the church

- the number of divorces among congregants

- the number of serious friendships developing among congregants

- people's desire to go overseas on short-term missions projects

- the level of spiritual sophistication observed by small group overseers

One desired outcome mentioned by only one pastor—but which seems critical for success—was that Christians experience the joy of growth. "Are they enjoying it? Because at the end of the day, if the people are saying, 'Man, this last year was like boot camp; I'm sure glad it's over,' then they're never going to do it again. If that happens, then we really haven't achieved our goal because our aim, as the Westminster Catechism would teach it, is to glorify God and enjoy Him forever."

This pastor serves a church in the Southeast that is constantly refining its process but has exploded with growth over the last twenty years. "[We're looking for people to say] 'I am enjoying and delighting in doing. I love this discipleship stuff. I love getting to know more about Christ, about who He is, and I'm going to go out and get other people to come into my group next year because it is so good. I loved doing this and I want more people to do it with me next year.' That would probably be the ultimate mark of success for us."

There are, of course, a variety of personal indicators of growth that this church encourages people to rely on. These include:

- self-evaluations of how they are doing in reaching their predetermined spiritual goals

- discussions with family and small group members regarding progress

- filling out church-developed or standardized assessment tools

- regular advisory sessions with more-mature Christians to discuss growth patterns and experiences

- encouraging people to journal and to review previous journal entries to sense progress or barriers

- challenging people to identify ways in which they apply the lessons from recent sermons

- reflective prayer, seeking direct revelation from God as to what is and is not working in the discipleship efforts

As a general guideline, we discovered that the typical disciple devotes an average of four to six hours per week, beyond attending the worship service, to spiritual development efforts.

Inclusiveness

Some of the successful churches we studied invite everyone to get involved in a full-fledged discipleship program (whether they are saved or not), while others make discipleship one of the benefits available to believers. The general consensus was that somewhere in the neighborhood of 50 to 65 percent of the congregation's adults were presently involved in a serious process of spiritual development. The low end of the scale was 40 percent; the upper end was 80 percent.

These figures were based upon some fairly demanding measures

of consistent commitment to growth. Worthy o.
that the pastors we talked to had a very solid unde
percentage of adults who were involved in a discip
When we quizzed them as to the basis of the figu
using, each offered solid, substantive reasons for the ngures they
were suggesting. The implication: *Successful pastors care about the
discipleship commitment of their people, they monitor it closely, and
they respond when the numbers suggest a waffling of dedication to spiritual advancement.*

*Not one of the highly effective churches waits
until a person is eighteen or twenty-one to begin
an intensive, intentional discipling process.*

Another key to disciple building is starting the process before a
person reaches adulthood. Not one of the highly effective churches
waits until a person is eighteen or twenty-one to begin an intensive,
intentional discipling process. Each church has its own starting
point and reasons for why they start at that age. One church begins
kids in preschool with a regimen of principles (based on stories) and
practices (group activities) that fits within a long-term plan for spiritual development. We encountered at least one disciple-making
church that initiates the process at any grade level between the first
and ninth grades. Most impressive was the fact that each church
had a reason—usually based on developmental psychology or other
behavioral and educational research—as to why they begin the
process at a particular age or grade level. Clearly, this is a matter that

.eceived much thought and testing with the goal of maximizing the potential for growing genuine followers of Christ.

COORDINATING THE ACTIVITIES

About half of these churches coordinate all of the church teaching and activity across age groups. In other words, the substantive focus of the church during any given week is coordinated around a particular principle, Bible passage, or developmental theme. The coordination includes the sermon topic, Sunday school lessons, small group lessons, church prayer meetings, and special community service options.

About one-quarter of the churches coordinate these elements within specific age groupings. For example, all adult activities and all children's activities will be content-coordinated, although the content might not be the same in the adult program as in the children's program. The most common reason for this separation is the difficulty of keeping young people and older people moving at the same pace and emphasizing the same topics while maintaining churchwide enthusiasm for the process and its substance.

THE DRIVING FORCE

In the highly effective disciple-making churches, the senior pastor was acknowledged to be the catalyst behind the commitment to spiritual growth. In most cases the day to day management of the process has been handed over to someone on staff or to an elder or other lay leader. However, most of the people we interviewed suggested that it is the passion of the senior pastor that prevents the church from becoming lazy in this dimension of ministry.

The role of the pastor in disciple making is usually one of providing vision and motivation to the congregation and ensuring that the resources are available to carry on the ministry. In other words, these pastors truly function as leaders—individuals who motivate people on the basis of a vision for discipleship, mobilize them to engage in purposeful participation, provide general direction for the process, and supply the resources necessary to get the job done. Often after the pastor delivers such leadership, the process continues to run smoothly under the supervision of skilled individuals who have "bought into" the vision and become its advocates.

For context, we also interviewed pastors and leaders in many churches that are not doing well in discipleship. In almost every case, we learned that either the senior pastor is silent about discipleship or merely gives lip service to its importance.

METHODS OF EFFECTIVE DISCIPLESHIP

Among the highly effective churches, no two had exactly the same delivery methods in place. Among the common methods were:

- small groups

- sermons tied to practical applications and a long-term plan of specific content to be delivered

- new-believer classes

- leadership training programs

- one-to-one mentoring

- Bible memorization

- Sunday school classes (classes that progressively help people develop a more comprehensive and integrated worldview)

- community service ministry groups

- online curriculum

- "mini-church" events

- two- and three-year classes on worldview foundations

- daily Bible reading programs

- a wide variety of ministry events

- book discussion groups

- life plan development

- spiritual gift assessment and activation

- a large-group discipleship training process (that is, a typical classroom instruction approach)

What Didn't Work

It may be helpful to identify some of the developmental approaches that typically failed to produce the desired results. Flawed approaches included the following:

- trying to produce disciples without first having a clear, crisp, and compelling definition of discipleship

- using discipleship curriculum developed by any of the large, highly regarded churches

- doing discipleship activities without having a well-conceived, long-term discipleship strategy as the foundation for decision making, resource allocation, and ministry implementation

- using small groups as a forum for evangelism

- emphasizing biblical knowledge without a complementary emphasis upon behavioral change

Helpful and Not-So-Helpful Resources

When it came to specific resources, few existing tools proved to be very helpful to the disciple-making efforts. Most of the materials these churches use were developed in-house. However, some churches described these tools as useful additions to the materials and resources they had created:

- topical small-group materials from a range of organizations and individuals (including Willow Creek, Serendipity, the Navigators, Kay Arthur, and Beth Moore)

- *The Purpose-Driven Church* by Rick Warren

- *Experiencing God* by Henry Blackaby and Claude King

- daily devotional guides, especially when tied to other church-driven content

Among the available tools that were generally panned by these churches were standardized curriculum (disparaged by pastors as too generic, too rigid, too linear, and boring), videos (deemed potentially useful as discussion starters but useless as teaching supplements if longer than ten minutes), and standardized evangelism programs (too hokey, often focused on techniques rather than hearts).

About half of these churches use events successfully to motivate people to engage in discipleship or to further their development. About one-quarter have tried various events but abandoned the practice after finding them to be fruitless. The remaining one-quarter have avoided events altogether based on a philosophical concern about reliance upon them. Among the events that have produced good results for the event-using churches were Vacation Bible School, community service outreaches, small-group introductory events, relationship-building activities, and family development adventures.

Small Groups

Perhaps the most popular tactic is to motivate people to join a small group within which to experience a more personal discipling environment. Although a handful of these churches tried small groups and disbanded them because they did not generate the desired results, most others consider these small, home-based, church-directed aggregations to be the cornerstone of their development process. However, most of the churches also acknowledge that unless there is ample training for facilitators, a tight accountability process, strong relational connections, and a purposeful selection of material to cover, the small groups will fail to produce disciples. Most of these churches establish groups that run for an academic year (September through June), are disbanded for the summer, then may re-form for the next academic year.

Sunday school classes are most commonly used by Southern Baptist churches in their discipleship efforts. Relatively few of the other highly effective disciple-making churches we studied rely upon Sunday school classes for adults; most, however, do use such classes for the shaping of young people. A popular adult alternative is the Adult Bible Fellowship (ABF) used in several of the congregations. An ABF is essentially a content-heavy, midsized teaching experience in which a collection of small groups, comprising anywhere between thirty to eighty people, meets together each Sunday morning before or after the worship service. The primary purpose of the ABF is to give people high-quality Bible teaching. Each ABF is taught the same material in any given week, and the content is related to that week's sermon. This frees small groups to discuss applications, implement accountability, and develop more intimate relationships. The ABF approach typically is used in tandem with small groups, serving as a segue from the large group, worship-driven experience in the sanctuary to the intimacy and lifestyle-transformation orientation of the small group.

> *Unless there is ample training for facilitators, a tight*
> *accountability process, strong relational connections,*
> *and a purposeful selection of material to cover,*
> *the small groups will fail to produce disciples.*

Many churches also rely upon topical Christian education classes designed to fill in the gaps of people's spiritual understanding, to polish skills they want to hone, or to introduce them to matters that they think might be of value or interest but will not be touched upon in their other discipleship venues. The topics covered in such classes run the gamut from learning Greek and Hebrew to discovering how to study the Bible or how to befriend non-Christians. Few of the churches we studied consider these classes integral elements of the disciple-making process; the classes are more of a community service than a core component. In a few churches, such topical courses were offered as the summertime replacement for the small groups that do not meet during July and August.

MENTORING AND COACHING

Most of the highly effective disciple-making churches integrate mentoring or coaching into their process. The ways in which this happens vary tremendously. Some churches raise up future leaders and teachers by having them serve as apprentices to church staff. Other congregations have more traditional one-to-one matches, with one individual serving as the discipler and the other as the disciple. Some churches modify that approach and use an "account-ability partner" model: Both people are on equal footing, meeting regularly to talk, pray, and encourage each other spiritually. Several congregations use a trickle-down model: A staff person mentors a half-dozen laypeople, each of those people mentor from two to six other congregants, and each of those people does the same.

All of the churches we studied were sold on the value of mentoring; only one church reported having a "bad experience" and had abandoned the practice. The toughest jobs, we discovered, are training people to be effective mentors (not everyone is good at this, of course), knowing how to integrate someone into the flow when he or she is not a skilled mentor (and does not possess much mentoring potential), keeping people's time commitments up to snuff, and preventing the mentoring process from becoming strictly a fellowship effort.

Few churches use the Internet for anything more than an information dumping ground; we did not discover any innovative or productive uses of the Net for discipleship. A handful of churches try to shake up the predictability of the process by using a tape, book, or other outside resource as a focal point for interaction among people. (This is done in different ways: Encouraging people to get the resource and engage someone in conversation about it, inviting people to a churchwide event to interact on that resource, and so forth.)

KEEPING PEOPLE MOTIVATED

Every church struggles with the challenge of motivating people to get involved and to stay involved in discipleship. Even people who enjoy the process and realize how beneficial it is go through periods when the pressures of life obscure the sense of value and fulfillment that comes from intimacy with God. How do effective churches handle such challenges?

One of the most common approaches we found was that of empowering people to challenge one another once they have developed trust-based relationships. Small groups have been good vehicles for facilitating this outcome. Pastors noted that when their peers are growing, people feel unstated pressure to stay focused on growth. There is a tremendous uplifting in the company of other believers who are also striving to grow. Being encouraged and guided by one's spiritual family is a powerful catalyst to perpetual effort, if not to constant development.

Most highly effective ministries also encourage people to put reasonable pressure on themselves to grow by having them identify their personal growth goals for the year. The beauty of this approach is that individuals cannot reject the goals as having been imposed by someone else. Because they've designated the desired outcomes of their own free will, they cannot blame anyone else for the challenges those goals present. Most churches we studied even have disciples sign a commitment form in relation to their objectives, and some provide quarterly or semiannual assessments of progress to help keep one another on track.

Many of these churches incorporate testimonies and other "success stories" into the church's regular events (for example, worship services). One purpose of these interviews and monologues is to encourage those exposed to the success of peers to sustain their commitment to growth. "Sometimes people just get tired or feel like they can't climb the hill," related one pastor who has a five-minute slot in each weekly worship service for a personal testimony by a teenager or adult. "But when they see Jennifer or Max stand up there—they know these people—and hear what God is doing through them, largely through perseverance, then everyone rethinks their own struggles and realizes, 'Man, if Max can do that, I bet I can too.' We're not making heroes out of these people, but just showing what happens when you stick to it and allow God to change you—no matter how inferior or incapable you feel."

THE INDISPENSABLE RESOURCES

Various resources were listed as indispensable for successful discipleship by the leaders of these churches. High-quality, well-trained leaders was the most frequently mentioned need. Passion for Christ and to live like Him were close seconds—and instigating such a desire is also largely a leadership function. Vision and clarity of purpose were deemed necessary by most churches, along with a churchwide commitment to Scripture, opportunities to build meaningful relationships that lead to accountability, and ample opportunities to use one's gifts.

All of the resources typically required to run a successful program were not thought of as relevant in regard to an effective discipleship ministry.

It may be equally instructive to note the resources that were *not* listed by these two dozen churches. Among them were: money, staff, facilities, and curriculum. In other words, *all of the resources typically required to run a successful program were not thought of as relevant in regard to an effective discipleship ministry.* It is a lay-driven endeavor that demands a culture of commitment, responsibility, and growth. This requires leadership, desire, and perseverance more than a bank account, a paid staff, or a central meeting place.

SUCCESSFUL PASTORS' ADVICE TO OTHERS

The pastors of the highly effective disciple-making churches are well aware that the level of productivity they have fostered is not the norm. Many have labored at other churches, or even at their present church, under circumstances that are similar to that of most churches. They comprehend the magnitude and the nature of the challenge facing most churches. What would they recommend to other pastors and leaders who are interested in upgrading their level of discipleship? To follow is a summary of the advice they gave:

- *Recognize that disciple making is a process, not a program.* It is about building people, not creating methods and systems. More important than anything else is to develop a churchwide culture that esteems becoming a disciple.

- *The process will not occur without leadership from the senior pastor.* Motivating widespread and diligent participation cannot be delegated to a staff person or lay leader. They may be able to move the process forward, but they will not get the process off the ground. The weight of the senior leader's commitment to personal spiritual growth is required to initiate the process.

- *The church's ministry focus must be streamlined to prioritize and support discipleship.* That includes establishing genuine spiritual growth as a core element of the church's mission, providing a clear definition of discipleship, instituting a compelling motivation for involvement, eliminating programs and ministries that divert people's attention and the church's resources, determining the practical realities of facilitating spiritual transformation, and creating dynamic means of enabling people to grow.

- *The process is not likely to succeed unless there is a simple but intelligent plan for growth.* That plan must include measurable objectives and be consistently promoted and worked through by the church's leaders.

- *The process will not generate true disciples unless it has a designated supervisor to facilitate progress, foster creative problem solving and development, and strive for reasonable outcomes.* Setting out to realize growth goals that are too substantial, too sophisticated, and that must happen too quickly will produce discouragement and failure. Start small, experimenting with your process to see what works best within your culture. Let those disciples then become not only your "trophies," but also your advocates of effective disciple making. Establish reasonable outcomes that are challenging but achievable. Becoming a disciple is a lifelong process; transitioning your people from ministry observers and consumers into true disciples will not be accomplished overnight.

- *In creating a process that works, adapt lessons learned by other effective disciple-making churches to your own unique ministry context.* There's no sense in re-creating the wheel, but there's also no wisdom in simply copying what another church has done in a different ministry context. Use the principles they have learned to further your own efforts, but adapt them to the uniquenesses of your people.

- *Be prepared for burnout and complacency to set in after two or three years of involvement in an intensive process.* This tendency to depart from the process can be diffused by building a ministry environment in which almost everyone is involved in discipleship, in which leaders do not accept any excuses for a desire to depart from the process, and in which the culture demands consistent participation in spiritual-growth activities.

- *Carefully balance the competing interests of flexibility and structure.* People need to be motivated and organized, but they also need room to develop procedures that reflect who they are, where they are going, and what will generate the best results. Achieving and maintaining that balance necessitates strong, competent leadership. If leaders are going to err in fostering that balance, they should err on the side of demanding biblical substance and clear, unified direction.

NO EASY TASK

Let me close this chapter with two cautions. First, you may read the keys presented in this chapter and nod your head approvingly, as if you've heard this all before (you probably have) and as if it's no big deal. That's where you're wrong. This is a big deal. For these churches to have not only gathered the knowledge of what it takes to disciple people, but to have changed their church's heartbeat in order to facilitate life transformation in the prescribed ways is breathtaking. Many pastors and church leaders have the knowledge, but very few are implementing that information in ways that produce true disciples. Do not minimize the significance of the connection between knowledge and practice. What these churches are doing is profound.

Second, realize that, like your church, these churches face daily barriers to success in disciple making. The dominant obstacles they identified will be familiar to you: people's time pressures; the lack of motivation to become Christlike; cultural and demographic differences that preclude one-size-fits-all programs from working; the tendency to give up midway through a taxing process; internal competition with other church activities and programs; negative preconceived notions about "discipleship," reliance upon strict linear learning patterns; the lack of role models; narcissism, hardened hearts, and cheap grace; the church's program orientation; and people's belief that such an effort will produce no significant results. Do these roadblocks sound familiar?

The leaders of these churches pointed out that we are ministering to different people with different needs in a different culture than we were ten years ago. People are used to changing plans on a moment's notice, so getting long-term, inflexible commitments from disciples is tougher. We are drenched in information, so our information absorption and analysis skills have changed significantly. Technology, performance pressures, and lifestyle shifts have isolated individuals, causing them to be more open to relationships developed through church connections. Having been burned time after time, people are more suspicious of offers of a quick fix, and they also demand persuasive demonstrations of relevance prior to making any commitment. We have less of a knowledge base to build upon and must provide depth within the context of experience.

> *We are ministering to different people with different needs in a different culture than we were ten years ago.*

The experiences of these highly effective churches remind us not to fall prey to comfortable assumptions such as "All it takes is good preaching to produce true disciples," "Using the best curriculum money can buy will grow people spiritually," "Hiring competent staff is sufficient to move the process along," or "Placing a large proportion of people in small groups generates true disciples." These assumptions are inaccurate more often than they prove to be true.

Keep your eyes on the goal: We are dedicated to producing genuine followers of Jesus Christ. That demands that we help people develop a biblical worldview and a compassionate heart. Highly effective disciple-making churches dwell on how they can direct peoples' minds, hearts, and energy toward being devoted to a transformed life. They are not perfect churches, and they do not have perfect disciples. But they're getting closer to those outcomes day by day, by virtue of their clearly articulated, single-minded devotion to growing true disciples.

CHAPTER SEVEN

FIVE MODELS OF EFFECTIVE DISCIPLESHIP

Each model has great potential to produce zealots for Christ—people who "get it" and who live it.

As we studied the churches that are developing passionate, mature followers of Jesus Christ, I noticed five particular approaches that facilitate effective disciple making. While the approaches have many similarities, they also have some unique twists that qualify them as different models. In this chapter I want to share with you a brief overview of each model and why I believe each has resulted in effective discipleship.

For the sake of distinguishing these models in the course of this discussion, I will use the following names:

1. The *Competencies* Model, used at Pantego Bible Church[1]

2. The *Missional* Model, practiced at Fellowship Bible Church of Little Rock[2]

3. The *Neighborhood* Model, created by Perimeter Church[3]

4. The *Worldview* Model, originated by Fellowship Bible Church North[4]

5. The *Lecture-Lab* Model, developed by North Coast Church[5]

> *All five models emphasize enabling people to think and act like Christians.*

After reading this chapter you may wish to obtain further information about the strategies and resources these churches have found effective in their disciple-making process. In the notes section at the end of this book you will find Web site addresses for the above churches; I encourage you to investigate those sites for additional details and insights.

All five models emphasize enabling people to think and act like Christians. All five focus on character development, thinking and decision making, and building affirming relationships. The differences lie in how each model accomplishes those common objectives. My observation is that all five models have great potential to produce zealots for Christ—people who "get it" and who live it. Let's take a brief look at each approach.[6]

THE COMPETENCIES MODEL

This model is a highly integrated approach to discipleship that stands out in its emphasis on personal assessment and integration with all aspects of the ministry. The model is based on the Great Commandment and the Great Commission and broken into thirty specific competencies: *ten core beliefs, ten core practices,* and *ten core virtues.* The process considers these thirty dimensions in light of one's relationship with God and with other people:

This model requires the substantive integration of everything

10 Core Beliefs	10 Core Practices	10 Core Virtues
the Trinity	worship	joy
salvation by grace	prayer	peace
authority of the Bible	single-mindedness	faithfulness
personal God	Bible study	self-control
identity in Christ	total commitment	humility
church	biblical community	love
humanity	give away your time	patience
compassion	give away your money	integrity
eternity	give away your faith	kindness
stewardship	give away your life	gentleness

the church does. The worship services provide inspiration to become disciples, and the sermons are built around the thirty core competencies. People receive their primary theological instruction in a modified Sunday school/Adult Bible Fellowship process in which several small groups from a particular geographic area are combined into a learning community. These groups have a trained lay pastor, encompass thirty to fifty people, and meet every Sunday morning at the church campus to discuss the sermon topic.

Individuals then become active in ministry by belonging to a small group of ten to twelve people; groups are based on geographic and life-stage similarities, such as young married couples or empty nesters. The dominant function of that group is to be a biblical community—putting into practice the information and principles learned in the larger-group events. Small groups have a trained leader and are held accountable for specific outcomes related to service, evangelism, learning, and care giving.

The Christian Life Profile

Each individual is expected to not only engage with the congregation through the worship service, the midsized teaching community, and the small group, but also to commit to personal development in specific competencies. The areas of competence that most need attention are identified through the annual use of a personal spiritual evaluation tool called the Christian Life Profile, which contains 120 questions (four items per competency). In addition, three other individuals in the small group complete an abbreviated version of the assessment evaluating each individual's virtues. The results give the individual a sense of where personal spiritual formation may be most lacking. The small group then provides prayer support and encouragement throughout the year as the individual strives to improve in those weaker areas.

The results of a person's assessment are not compared with those of other individuals but serve as self-regulating indicators of personal strengths and weaknesses. Over time, as the individual completes several of these assessments, the results become a personal trend line marking relative growth or stagnation. The profile helps the individual focus on his or her spiritual condition and facilitates an appropriate domain of spiritual formation emphasis.

In addition, the church offers a range of topical classes that deal with the competencies. Nobody is required to attend these classes, but individuals who wish to develop in specific areas and who need more focused instruction may take advantage of the classes.

Thus every week it is possible for an individual to have five different church-based experiences that focus on the core competencies. The first is the sermon; the second is the midsized learning community; the third is the small group; the fourth is a weekly study guide that contains a daily reading, study, and application component; and the fifth is a specialized class available during the week at the church. Few people exploit all of these opportunities every week, but the concept of tying together so many interwoven elements to guide an individual along an intentional developmental path—with a similarly integrated and focused assessment instrument—is unique and effective.

The Competencies Model does not use events. This model

also minimizes other church programs and specialized ministries in favor of accomplishing all ministry through these existing avenues.

Pros and Cons of the Competencies Model

One of the major benefits of this model is its use of an objective and focused measurement strategy that is the total responsibility of the individual believer. Linking the entire ministry to a defined set of core competencies also makes something that feels amorphous —for example, biblical truth, spiritual development, life transformation—tangible and addressable. The measurement process and the thirty competencies provide congregants with a more extensive sense of belonging and purposeful community. The aggregate integration of all ministry aspects at the church sharpens the entire ministry effort and promotes more efficient spiritual growth on both a personal and corporate level. The integration of content also provides a built-in incentive to track with the worship services: Missing a weekend makes it difficult to keep up with the process.

The primary concerns related to this model emanate from the foundational tool, the Christian Life Profile. One concern is the reality of limiting the evaluation of one's performance in a core competency to four measurement questions: Can your integrity or love or humility really be assessed in just four queries? There is tremendous value in being able to examine personal maturity specifically and quantitatively, but you have to wonder if the instrument is sufficiently comprehensive or sensitive to do justice to a person's development.

Second, the "one another assessment," in which a person's peers from the small group evaluate his or her virtues, is of questionable validity. The concept is reasonable, but the accuracy of such measures is suspect. (For instance, do three people in your small group have enough exposure to your life to accurately rate how well you follow the Ten Commandments? Do they spend enough time observing your life to know if, when pressure hits, you always place your decisions before God?)

Finally, this process raises the challenge of how to handle success. The more mature people become, the more aware they are of their frailties in a particular area of development. Consequently, their self-assessment scores may decline at the very same time that their maturity is increasing. This could have the effect of discouraging believers or causing them to focus on a spiritual dimension of their life that is not as underdeveloped as a dimension that achieved a higher score precisely because the person was too underdeveloped in that dimension to realize the extent of his or her weakness.

THE MISSIONAL MODEL

This approach reflects a mixture of components found in the other models described in this chapter, specifically the Competencies and Worldview Models. The Missional Model was not developed with those in mind but evolved after experimentation and philosophical fine-tuning. The similarity to the other effective models is, of course, no accident: Shaping people's lives requires certain emphases as found in this and the other models described here.

I've labeled this the Missional Model—it is my name for their process, not a name the church adopted—because the approach is so closely tied to the church's mission. Their mission is to help people become spiritually mature as manifested in six core qualities or competencies:

1. being passionately committed to Jesus Christ

2. evaluating everything in their lives according to biblical standards

3. being deeply committed to having a healthy family

4. being morally pure

5. being evangelistically bold

6. being socially responsible and impactful

To facilitate such disciples, this model begins by introducing people to the fundamentals of the faith through a class that meets at the church for eight consecutive Sunday evenings. During the class, participants form various small groups consisting of ten to fourteen people. They also are introduced to the Personal Development Plan (PDP), a tool that helps them determine which of the six outcomes they want to focus on, what they will do during the coming year to achieve those outcomes, and how the results can be measured. (The church calendar is developed a year in advance to enable people to create a stable plan of activity.) Once the personal plan is developed, the individual shares it with the others in his or her small group. The group then encourages and prays for one another throughout the year in their efforts to grow in their areas of emphasis.

In the Missional Model, small groups are the focal point of personal growth. As such, every person who becomes a member/ adherent of the church is required to be in a small group. The groups meet every other week. Every individual in each group is responsible for developing and implementing a PDP. Groups typically are formed around common life stages or "seasons of life," such as groups for singles, young marrieds without children, parents with young families, and empty nesters.

To address the issue of burnout, the model incorporates two types of groups: standard small groups geared to personal development and ministry groups geared to external service and outreach. The model thus far has found that people stay in the personal-growth groups approximately three years before gravitating to the service-driven groups. It is in the outreach-oriented groups that people use their spiritual gifts to serve within the church or community or to address social issues from a faith perspective.

In addition to the small groups, the church provides a menu of specialty classes that are intimately related to the six core, missional qualities. Some of the classes consist of expositional teaching, some are theological in nature, and some are practical or skill-oriented. There are no Sunday school classes or midsized groups involved in this model. Special events are occasionally used to supplement the content and experiences people receive in their small groups or from special classes. By the way, every specialized ministry within the church is linked to the missional objectives. The preaching on weekends is worldview-oriented but not particularly tied to the activities of groups.

> *One of the most appealing aspects*
> *of the Missional Model is its simplicity.*

The Missional Model process is implemented starting in the first grade. Teachers identify specific objectives drawn from the missional outcomes that will be accomplished by each student during the year. Classroom and youth group activities are then developed around those objectives. As the kids enter their teen years they are encouraged to become involved in small groups and to become plan-directed.

Pros and Cons of the Missional Model

One of the most appealing aspects of the Missional Model is its simplicity. It takes planning, anticipation, resources, and a clear mission, but the process itself is easy for everyone to understand and implement.

Another advantage is that this approach is self-directed. Once people have been walked through the process of developing their

PDP and have become involved in a small group, they are essentially responsible for their own growth. There are small group leaders and other process managers who track progress and keep the momentum flowing, but the burden is mostly on the shoulders of the church members to make this process work. The PDP itself is a very positive tool for focusing people's attention on measurable outcomes to which they are committed.

A substantial benefit of this model is that it is very responsive to the needs of the congregation. Once congregants have taken a measure of where they stand in relation to the missional objectives and have then crafted a personal plan for growth, that information forms the basis of the church's programming for the coming year. In other words, once the church identifies the desired outcomes through the mission statement and the people describe what they need to manifest those behaviors, then the church provides the resources required to facilitate such outcomes.

The other advantage of this model is the fact that the missional objectives permeate everything within the ministry. Those six outcomes are few enough in number to be manageable, specific enough to be measurable, and compelling enough to be marketable to congregants.

The model does not place as much weight on exposing everyone to core theological foundations as do some other models. The introduction disciples receive is solid but brief; they will be exposed to additional related insights over time through courses, sermons, and discussions, but that process is not as central as in a few of the other models. And even though there is great freedom and wisdom in having people responsible for their personal growth evaluation, there will be a tendency for some people to exploit the subjective nature of those assessments to get by without truly pushing themselves.

THE NEIGHBORHOOD MODEL

The Neighborhood Model includes some of the elements seen in the Worldview, Competencies, and Missional Models, although it was developed independently of those approaches. And again, the name of this model is employed in this book for descriptive purposes, but it is not a title recognized by the church that created the model.

Here's how this one works. People new to the church might attend an inquirer's class to gain a general overview of the church. Once they decide they want to get serious about involvement, they join a neighborhood congregation, which is a group of fifteen to twenty people from the same general geographic location. That group will meet twice each month. One meeting focuses on worship, teaching, and fellowship; the other meeting focuses mainly on fellowship, with members encouraged to invite guests. (Members can invite guests to either meeting.) The group is led by a lay pastor who has received extensive preparation via a pastoral training process complete with qualifying tests, classroom teaching, textbooks, written tests, and oral examinations. The neighborhood congregation is the church's primary delivery point for spiritual nurture and care. It is also the main launching pad for outreach opportunities. Multiple neighborhood congregations are linked together for outreach activities, such as concerts, at the church.

Members of the geographic units are then encouraged to get involved in a more intensive discipling environment by joining a discipleship team. Each discipler leads five to nine individuals of the same gender through the developmental process. The focus of those efforts is twofold. First, each participant begins the year by creating a personal life plan. The plan defines the person's mission, vision, values, goals, and schedule for pursuing desired growth outcomes. That plan also identifies how the individual will strive to mature in five specific areas:

1. Bible knowledge

2. practical ministry skills

3. outreach

4. prayer

5. accountability

Then the disciples are led through a church-authored discipleship curriculum, which runs on a three-year cycle divided into six six-week modules per year. (The ministry year coincides with the academic year: September through May.) The disciplers are trained in how to lead the curriculum on a week-by-week basis, with leadership training occurring Sunday mornings at the main campus prior to the worship services. Consequently, every discipleship group is covering the same material in a given week. At the end of each ministry season, discipled individuals reevaluate their growth in accordance with their preset goals.

> *The Neighborhood Model takes both a systematic and practical approach to theology.*

To facilitate impact and the efficient use of human resources, individuals being discipled sign a covenant committing to one year of participation. They may choose to return after the year expires, but their disciplers must approve their return based on how well they satisfied their commitment. Once a person has gone through the three-year curriculum cycle, he or she is expected to graduate from *being discipled* to *becoming a discipler* of others. A key component of the Neighborhood Model is that it takes both a systematic and practical approach to theology, alternating between the two every six weeks. A heavy emphasis is placed on modeling evangelism.

Generally speaking, the sermons in the weekend worship services provide people with biblical content but are not aligned with the small group content. This model makes no use of Sunday school classes, although any classes that exist may be used to move people into the discipleship process. Special classes are typically offered throughout the year, giving people a chance to take highly focused courses on specialized theological topics. In-house events are also scheduled throughout the year to both recruit more disciples and to provide ministry skills such as evangelism training.

Pros and Cons of the Neighborhood Model

This model covers the bases of both inreach and outreach. The standardized three-year curriculum guarantees that the church can manage the flow of content and deliver an intentional biblical worldview tableau for people to examine. The inclusion of the personal life plan at the front end of the discipleship process appropriately places the responsibility for growth on the shoulders of the laity. That plan helps narrow each participant's focus to the specific outcomes that the model embraces. The Neighborhood Model also provides excellent front-end and ongoing training of leaders to perform their duties.

A disadvantage of this model includes the time commitment required for it to work. In addition to the weekend worship service, there are at least two additional meetings during the week plus time needed to complete related tasks and homework. The curriculum essentially assumes a fairly hefty rewrite every three years—which is a significant drain on church resources.

The Neighborhood Model also assumes that anyone who has completed the three-year cycle is ready to disciple other people. Given the variety of gifts, life stages, and temperaments resident within the church, maturity may not always mean that a person who is competent at understanding and living the Christian faith will also be proficient at teaching and coaching others.

THE WORLDVIEW MODEL

The primary thrust of the Worldview Model is the impartation of biblical wisdom that leads to personal transformation. This model is designed to increase people's participation in the church, to upgrade their level of service to other people, and to improve their ability to understand issues and make decisions from a biblical perspective. The primary objective of this process is to encourage people to think and behave biblically—in other words, to adopt a truly biblical worldview.

The model relies upon a two-year process that gives groups of people a thorough grounding in the foundational truths of Christianity. These groups are open to anyone who wants to grow in spiritual maturity. (A significant proportion of those involved are nonbelievers who often accept Christ as their Savior during the initial phase of the process.) Because the establishing process is so central in the aggregate ministry and life of the church, sermons often encourage people to take spiritual maturity seriously and to enroll in the discipleship process.

> *The Worldview approach is based on confronting learners with dissonance.*

The discipleship curriculum, known as The Discovery Series, encompasses four topical books requiring an average of sixty to ninety minutes per week in personal reading, study, and reflection in addition to the time spent in Discovery class. This curriculum covers an exhaustive spectrum of basic theological and doctrinal issues that includes conversion, baptism, the work of the Holy Spirit, prayer, church involvement, Satan, the nature of God, community, service, world impact, evangelism, and apologetics. The class is dialogical rather than lecture-driven, and the precepts are embraced through a combination of Bible study and guided group discussion rather than accepting authoritative claims made by an expert teacher. Group members are given the opportunity to work out their questions and applications in the presence of others who are struggling with similar issues. The Worldview Model asks people to:

- identify the issue at hand

- study the Bible in relation to that issue

- gather wisdom from other sources

- make a personal response to the accumulated information

- discuss that response with the other members of the group

- develop personal strategies for living out the truth discovered

The Worldview approach is based on confronting learners with dissonance—asking them to wrestle with real-world problems and apply biblical principles to these problems. Dissonance is achieved through case studies, group discussion, and service projects. In my view, the process is akin to what Christian parents do with their children: Establish them in principles that will shape their values, beliefs, and behaviors, then release them to refine these principles in the real world—always with a strong support base (a small group) as their touchstone.

While students are completing the Discovery courses over a two-year period, they are also encouraged to deepen their spiritual maturity in the context of a small group. The purpose of these small groups is to continue to use the Bible study and life-learning skills developed in Discovery to experience the encouragement and accountability of intimate relationships and to engage in community service projects. Each small group has a trained lay leader, and there are also peer mentors who provide spiritual care for up to three individuals in the group.

The Worldview Model also uses special events, such as Walk Thru the Bible seminars, as feeder activities for the Discovery process. Advanced Christian education classes, such as book studies, topical studies, and leadership training, are offered throughout the year, but these serve as addenda to the main thrust of the process.

This model does not use a traditional Sunday school structure and does not integrate the Internet into the process.

Pros and Cons of the Worldview Model

The major benefit of this model is that it ensures that each individual has gone through a thorough process of learning fundamental spiritual truths and principles and received ample instruction in how to think and act biblically. The Discovery curriculum is well conceived and practical. The process of shifting Discovery graduates from a larger learning group to a smaller, more intimate group for continual application, encouragement, and accountability also works well.

The dominant weakness in the Worldview Model is the absence of effective assessment tools and measures at various points along the way. Another consideration is the necessity of the individual's devoting two years to the front end of the process before moving on. The conflict, of course, is this: On the one hand, people's lives often do not accommodate an intensive, two-year commitment, and on the other hand, providing a complete introduction to worldview thinking and the spectrum of core biblical doctrines is not likely to be adequately accomplished in less time.

THE LECTURE-LAB MODEL

This model focuses on delivering content through sermons (that is, lecture) and using small groups as the means of exploring the content further to follow through on applications (that is, the laboratory). The Lecture-Lab Model's bottom line is gleaning knowledge and building faith-based relationships that lead to godly character and Christian service. In this approach, the purpose of biblical knowledge is not to pass tests but to motivate people to live obedient lives, bear spiritual fruit, and persevere through the trials and tests of life. While Bible knowledge is not disparaged, it is not the primary building block in this approach. Rather it is the launching point of a multifaceted, coordinated developmental process.

> *The Lecture-Lab Model's bottom line is gleaning knowledge and building faith-based relationships that lead to godly character and Christian service.*

The sermons are expository but arranged in four- to twelve-week themed series. The pastor delivers each message in two major sections: (1) the background and principles imparted in the selected passage, and (2) challenges as to how to live a Christian life. The ultimate goal is to cover enough Bible principles so that, over the course of several years, people have been provided with sufficient content to grasp a biblical worldview and to understand how to make decisions on the basis of scriptural principles.

Each week people receive an outline to follow in the service along with "homework" related to the sermon presentation—related passages to read, specific verses to study, and questions to ponder—and an outline for the topic-related discussion that might take place in the small group. Within the small groups, trained leaders facilitate discussion, prayer, and accountability to help people use their gifts to serve others. One of the benefits of the Lecture-Lab Model is that questions that arise in response to the sermon can be dealt with among caring peers; the utility of the information taught in the weekend services can be scrutinized more deeply and more practically in small groups than in a general presentation to hundreds of people in an auditorium. The lab portion of the model is designed to encourage learners to personalize the insights and get feedback from group members on the personal application of the teaching.

The model requires that everything be Word-centered: the teaching, the relationships, the accountability process, and the service emphasis. Once the relationships take root and the group finds its stride in grappling with the teaching content, then the focus on application and accountability kicks in. Sunday school is not part of this strategy among the adults; for them, the small groups constitute the primary learning forum. Adolescents and teenagers tend to be integrated into the worship service and are also encouraged to be active in small groups (as well as midweek age-based youth groups). For the younger children, Sunday school classes remain a crucial part of the growth experience.

The small groups each have a leader who acts as facilitator but answers to a small-group supervisor. Each group has between ten and sixteen people and meets for a ten-week period. After the ten weeks, there is a brief hiatus after which people may rejoin their group or join another group that has openings. Upon entering a group, people sign a covenant to remain actively involved for the full ten-week period.

Group leaders are assigned by the church, based on their training and qualifications. There are different responsibilities for leaders and hosts, freeing the leader to focus on facilitating group interaction and growth. Leaders are responsible for submitting regular reports regarding attendance, major issues being addressed, and other key insights into the life and direction of the group. There are two levels of supervisors: those who oversee five group leaders and those who oversee twenty-five leaders. The most successful churches using this model have a regular reporting regimen, hold regular meetings and conversations between the various leaders, and offer scheduled training events.

Pros and Cons of the Lecture-Lab Model

From both a theological and service standpoint, the Lecture-Lab Model is the "loosest" or most casual of the five spiritual development approaches described in this chapter. That has many benefits as well as a few potential problems.

Among the benefits of this model are that the sermon becomes something more than a warm-and-fuzzy-but-forgettable message. Because the sermon material forms the substantive foundation of a second go-round for small group participants, the biblical principles imparted are hammered home at least twice. Similarly, by making the sermon the core content from which personal learning and applications spring, the church can ensure that over a limited time period everyone receives exposure to the basic components of a biblical worldview. Further, the emphasis upon the sermon content within small groups means that regular worship service attendance becomes more important. It is harder to be inconsistent in attending when your peers, who hold you accountable for growth, might confront you for your lax commitment to sharing the basic worship and teaching experience.

By using the sermon as the lecture content, the small group

leader need not be a strong Bible teacher, but he or she must be a skilled facilitator of conversation around a theme and the ancillary content provided by the church staff. This provides for a more relational experience and one not so utterly dependent upon the teaching preparation and gifts of the facilitator. This permits a large church to have more than a handful of well-led groups.

The small group emphasis makes relationships much more significant in the life of the church—which is a definite plus. It is those relationships that lead people to integrate spiritual growth into their lives in ways that make the process less intrusive and less overwhelming than might be experienced through a more overt process. The accountability process is more natural in the small-group environment, and the Lecture-Lab Model also fosters the expectation that people will identify their gifts and serve in connection with those gifts.

Clearly, the major downside of the model—but one that could be overcome without much difficulty—is the absence of any objective, broad-based evaluation system. The church does make some effort to determine the spiritual health of believers through head counts, ease of recruiting participants for ministry opportunities, and the usual anecdotal evidence. But a more reliable method of assessing spiritual development would enhance this model. A better evaluation method would be especially useful in gauging how well people understand and embrace a biblical worldview that drives their relationships, thinking, and behavior.

Another potential shortcoming of the Lecture-Lab Model is that it does not incorporate any type of broad-based introduction to basic knowledge about theology or doctrine. Such insights are available through occasional classes, but these are optional components that are not integral to the model. The danger, of course, is that people may enter the system without much background or comprehension of the Christian faith and have to play theological catch-up without systematic or intentional guidance in that effort.

USING THE NET

While the Internet does not play a significant role in the discipleship process of any of these highly effective churches, let me note that several of these congregations do use the Net as a backup system for individuals who missed weekend worship services. Through audio streaming of sermons and downloadable outlines and small group assignments, the churches make it possible for those who were absent, for whatever reason, to remain abreast of key information and materials.

A "BEST OF" MODEL

Each of these models has something unique and valuable to offer to our study of what makes a discipleship process effective. Each of these models is more sophisticated and productive than the discipleship process existing in most of the churches I have examined. Adapting any one of these models, as they stand, would significantly boost the overall quality of discipleship in the typical congregation in America. The Christian church would be radically impacted by a widespread commitment to any of these approaches to advancing people's spiritual maturity.

But let me throw another thought into the arena for your consideration. One of the practices I witness in every highly effective church I study is that they borrow great ideas from every place they find them. Highly effective churches have less of a sense of pride of ownership in their ideas and practices than a sense of pride in the quality of their ministry. They would rather borrow an idea from another ministry and adapt and refine it to their own unique circumstances than insist upon developing new ideas in isolation and ignorance.

> *One of the practices I witness in every highly effective church I study is that they borrow great ideas from every place they find them.*

Let me encourage you to follow that pattern of ministry by offering a hybrid model for your consideration. It is essentially a "Best of" model built by taking the stellar parts of the five models we just explored to create a new "supermodel"—with all due apologies to Claudia Schiffer, Tyra Banks, Cindy Crawford, and other reigning supermodels.

We must start with the realization that producing zealous and mature disciples of Jesus Christ requires a church culture in which the concepts and practice of discipleship permeate everything we do. What would that look like?

- The senior pastor of the church is an irrepressible advocate of discipleship.

- Church membership is granted only when a person covenants to participate in a focused, demanding discipleship process.

- All ministry programs are intimately tied to discipleship outcomes.

- The number of programs is minimized in order to focus the church's ministry on and through the discipleship process.

- All teaching in the church, from Sunday morning classes for elementary school children through the worship service and other adult teaching venues, is substantively coordinated.

- The church mission statement serves as a practical tool for identifying necessary ministry outcomes that are tied to an annually updated series of goals that directly relate to the mission statement and to the spiritual state of the congregation.

The process itself would begin with the use of personal evaluation tools (as found in the Competencies Model) and church outcomes assessment (as found in the Missional Model). The aggregate discipleship experience would be tied to the use of those tools.

After participating in a self-evaluation and goal-setting effort, individuals would be required to complete an intensive interactive course designed to ensure that they grasp the fundamentals of the faith (as delivered within the Worldview Model).

Upon completion of that activity, they would sign a short-term covenant with the church regarding their Personal Development Plan for that term. Ideally, covenant terms would last for an academic year (September through May).

As part of the covenant, participants would agree to engage in several activities. Among those would be a small group that meets in someone's home during the week, perhaps every other week. These meetings would be primarily for prayer, fellowship, accountability, and community service. Each small group would belong to a midsized congregation within the larger congregation, akin to the Adult Bible Fellowship structure. These midsized groups would meet every Sunday morning and provide both an expanded relational network as well as exposure to interactive teaching related to the week's sermon topic.

Every disciple would also be expected to regularly participate in the church's worship services and in community service options offered by the church. These options would facilitate people's spiritual development as well as the ministry impact of the church. In addition, each disciple would have a mature mentor who works with him or her on a regular basis, helping the disciple to remain focused on personal developmental objectives. At the end of each year, disciples would evaluate how they have done in relation to their predetermined spiritual goals for the year. Believers would develop their personal plan for the coming year in light of where they stand spiritually and what they have learned about their spiritual development capacity.

For the process to work best, all sermons preached throughout the year would relate to a planned schedule of worldview components. The idea would be to expose all disciples in the church to the building blocks of a Christian worldview within a two- or three-year window.

By the way, the same process that is utilized among adults would be used among children and teenagers. The underlying idea is to build a lifestyle of discipleship as soon as possible in a person's life. In addition, when everyone in a family is on the same spiritual development track, it becomes easier for the family to have a shared spiritual experience outside of church. Because it is the parents' responsibility to foster the spiritual maturity of their children, coordinating the church's discipleship track across all age groups would help parents be more effective in fulfilling this spiritual obligation.

You can fill in the cracks around this basic synthesis of ideas. Such a model, implemented as the foundation of your church's ministry, could work well regardless of the size of your church or its doctrinal leanings. If you don't particularly care for this model, perhaps it will stimulate you to develop your own approach to discipleship based on the strengths of the models we have explored.

CHAPTER EIGHT

GO, MARK DISCIPLES

———◆———

*When Jesus began His public ministry,
His top priority was to recruit
and train disciples.*

———◆———

Your church is involved in many activities and programs. A disciple-making ministry is probably among the plethora of ministries already in place. Isn't it enough just to make discipleship one of the many endeavors of the church?

Establishing priorities is one of the chief functions of a leader—and wisely choosing which endeavors should become dominant priorities distinguishes great leaders from also-rans. And here's a clue as to the relative importance of disciple making: When Jesus began His public ministry, what was His choice of priorities? His top priority was to recruit and train disciples. Although a variety of ministry components were important to Him—worship, evangelism, stewardship, passing on spiritual truths, building community, serving people—each of those was folded into His discipling process.

In many churches we fight internally over what should be the top ministry priority—worship, evangelism, Christian education, and so forth. In so doing we have unconsciously chosen the model of James and John—asking who will be first—rather than the model of Jesus—asking who wants to be whole. We continually engage in political and programmatic turf fights because we fail to understand that when we become true disciples of Christ such territorialism becomes superfluous. True disciples will integrate those functions and efforts into a seamless blend of faith-driven activity.

> *When Jesus began His public ministry,*
> *what was His choice of priorities? His top priority*
> *was to recruit and train disciples.*

Does that seem ideal or idealistic? I believe it is ideal and realistic, based on the experience of disciple-making churches. Sure, they have squabbles, but the infighting is less pronounced and less frequent. When we get our priorities right, everything falls into line. True discipleship must be a priority within the church. In fact, without a heavy emphasis upon discipleship, there is no church.

If we can read between the lines of Jesus' ministry, it appears that His underlying philosophy was to make disciples now, make them continually, and use whatever resources and opportunities were presently available for that purpose—but never, never stop molding people into Christlikeness. The Lord knew that when people become Christlike, the fundamental expressions of our faith will emerge naturally.

Let's Be Real

Truthfully, while disciple making must be a priority for you, by whatever means you select, you must enter the process with your eyes open. What happens when you make true disciples—not just students or group members, but genuine zealots for Christ?

- People's lives change.

- Society is changed by the disciples.

- Society experiences turmoil as a result of the church's being true to God's truths and commands.

- Disciples are persecuted.

Growing true disciples and being true disciples, while exhilarating, are not joyrides. Discipleship is not the answer to every cultural problem that exists—in fact, an effective discipleship process may create new tensions and animosities within the culture as God's principles clash with Satan's principles in the battle of spiritual kingdoms. But the hardships that arise as a result of engagement in disciple making are no excuse to avoid or minimize our devotion to the process and its outcomes. In fact, trials are an indicator that the church is being the church. As long as the battle between good and evil persists, we will not experience a peaceful, loving, wholly satisfying society. However, while being avid, passionate disciples of Jesus Christ will not bring about the perfect society, the thrust to be true disciples is the answer for each of us, individually, in the quest to become pleasing and honorable in God's sight.

> *The hardships that arise as a result of engagement*
> *in disciple making are no excuse to avoid or minimize*
> *our devotion to the process and its outcomes.*

We cannot help but have a positive impact on the world when we are being Christlike. However, we will not be loved and accepted by everyone. Not even Jesus, the Son of God, the Prince of Peace, the Savior of humankind, was loved by all people. If we follow His ways and His footsteps, we should not expect to be loved and accepted by everyone either. But God, the Father of Creation, was completely pleased with the work of the Son—and that was all that mattered to the Son. So Jesus is our model and that is our challenge: to gain the acceptance of the Father by imitating the work of the Son through the empowerment of the Spirit. That is a task clearly beyond our capabilities. The results are up to God.

LOOK FOR THE MARKS

When you hire people, you study their lives for clues as to what they will be like as employees. When you buy products, you study the contents and reviews to determine which products will provide the outcomes you desire. As you strive to become a disciple and to make disciples, keep your eyes on the marks of a true disciple:

- the passion of Stephen

- the joy of the post-Pentecost apostles

- the integrity of Nathanael

- the availability of Mary

- the perseverance of Paul

- the transformation of Peter

- the wisdom of James

- the servanthood of Martha

- the love of John

- the generosity of Joseph the Levite from Cyprus

- the seriousness of John the Baptist

- the studiousness of Luke

- the humility and reverent faith of the centurion

- the evangelistic sharing of Andrew

- the character of Jesus

None of these stalwarts of the faith (with the exception of Jesus) was a perfect representation of each of the qualities listed here. Each of these individuals stood out for a handful of qualities and presumably worked on developing other qualities that brought him or her into greater conformity with Jesus' life. As you study their paths to glory, keep in mind that even the models of our faith fell short of the glory of God. By our very nature, we always will, but by God's grace we must not accept our limitations as excuses to give up.

The real obstacles to becoming fully devoted, zealous disciples of Christ are not money, time, methods, or knowledge. The major obstacle is the human heart. When that changes, all else changes. Jesus frequently reminded His disciples that the problem was not one of knowledge but of character. The Pharisees had more religious knowledge than they knew what to do with, but they lacked the character to apply it in ways that transformed themselves and their world. Judas spent many months living with Jesus, observing His ways and His miracles, learning timeless and transforming principles directly from the lips of the Master, and yet all of His knowledge and experience could not compensate for a wicked heart. A disciple is a person of Christian character. Just as Paul instructed his young disciple Timothy, if you develop appropriate character, the rest will follow.

"Therefore Go..."

Be a true disciple. Go and make disciples. What will this look like, when it works?

- True discipleship produces holistic personal transformation, not mere assimilation into a community of church members.

- True discipleship is witnessed by people who are determined to be a blessing to others—people who are never content to simply accept and enjoy God's blessings.

- True discipleship creates Christians who aggressively pursue spiritual growth rather than passively experience spiritual evolution.

- True discipleship spawns individuals who develop renewed lifestyles instead of believers who mechanically check off completed assignments on a developmental agenda.

- True discipleship results in people who are more concerned about the quality of their character than the extent of their knowledge.

- True discipleship builds churches known for their culture of love, commitment, and service rather than for their events, information, and programs.

- True discipleship facilitates people devoted to a lifelong journey to imitate Jesus Christ rather than the completion of a short-term regimen of tasks and responsibilities.

> *Can we fulfill this mammoth challenge?*
> *Jesus, our mentor, says we can.*

Do you passionately want to become a zealous disciple of Jesus Christ? Are you committed to bring others with you on that amazing journey?

Discipleship is about complete obedience to the Word of God, driven by a heart that can stand to do nothing less and a mind that knows it pays to focus on nothing else. Can we fulfill this mammoth challenge? Jesus, our mentor, says we can. "I tell you the truth, anyone who has faith in me will do what I have been doing. He will do even greater things than these" (John 14:12).

If you are devoted to the process of spiritual growth and to allowing God's Holy Spirit to shape you on that journey, how you end up will bear scant resemblance to what you were when you began the journey.

May your journey be joyful and fruitful!

RESEARCH
METHODOLOGY

This book is based upon a number of research efforts related to discipleship and spiritual growth and among churches that engage in effective discipleship ministry. Here is an outline of the research projects conducted by the Barna Research Group from which the data in this book were derived.

SURVEYS AMONG ADULTS

All of the following were telephone surveys based upon nationwide random samples of adults living in the forty-eight continental states. The surveys were conducted from the Barna Research field center in southern California, and interviews were conducted on weeknights from 5 to 9 P.M., on Saturdays from 10 A.M. to 6 P.M., and on Sundays from noon through 8 P.M. (All times listed are the times in the time zone of the survey respondent.) The interviews analyzed in this book were divided among born-again Christian adults and non-born-again adults. The born-again adults were operationally defined as people who had made a personal commitment to Jesus Christ that is still important in their lives today and believe that after they die they will go to heaven only because they confessed their sins and have accepted Jesus Christ as their Savior.

Survey Field Dates	Born-Again	Not Born-Again
January–February 1999	405	597
November–December 1999	450	651
January–February 2000	417	585
May–June 2000	465	538

SURVEYS AMONG PASTORS

In addition to interviewing churched and unchurched adults, we also spoke with two samples of Protestant senior pastors. One survey was a national random sampling of 601 senior pastors conducted by telephone during June and July 2000. That survey was a representative sampling of Protestant churches and included questions pertaining to ministry to the unchurched.

The other study was among an elite sample of pastors and church leaders from congregations that are doing an outstanding job of building true disciples. The original sample list was developed from calls made to denominational executives, church consultants and analysts, and ministry specialists. From that list we then narrowed down the body of "qualified" churches to those that are doing unusually effective discipleship. That was determined by assessing the percentage of adults actively involved in a disciple-making capacity, the ministry emphasis placed upon discipleship, and the quality and quantity of changed lives resulting from the church's discipleship ministry. This portion of the research was qualitative and nonstatistical in nature, based on extensive interviews and evaluations of the churches' efforts to make disciples. The churches involved in this portion of the research came from every region of the country; represented more than a dozen Protestant denominations, mainline and evangelical; and averaged as few as 150 to as many as 4,500 adults attending the church on a typical weekend.

ADDITIONAL RESEARCH

This report also draws on information from other surveys we have recently conducted. Among them is a nationwide telephone survey of a random sample of 610 teenagers, conducted in October 1999.

NOTES

<hr/>

Chapter 1: Do You Want to Make a Difference?

1. It is not my contention that these are the only five discipleship models that truly work. However, after studying hundreds of churches from across the nation and seeking to identify those in which life transformation was a consistent product of the discipleship activities undertaken, these were the only five models that emerged. There were numerous other strategies and models we found in place at other churches, but those approaches produced students, members, registrants, or participants—not disciples.

Chapter Three: The State of Discipleship

1. Throughout this book, as in all of the research conducted by the Barna Research Group, the term "born-again Christian" will be used to denote people who have made a personal commitment to Christ that is important in their lives and who believe they will have eternal life because they have confessed their sins and accepted Jesus Christ as their Savior. We do not ask people to define themselves as born-again or indicate whether they have had a "born-again experience." Instead, after people respond to the two survey questions regarding personal commitment to Christ

and what they believe will happen to them after they die, we categorize the individual as born-again or not born-again. As of this writing, four out of ten adults and one out of three teenagers fit the born-again classification. Of course, only God truly knows who is and is not a Christian. The use of such research questions is not to condone or condemn people but to provide an estimation of what is happening in our culture and within the church.

2. The groups most desirous of such input were people in their thirties, those living in the South and Midwest, African-Americans, and people who are registered to vote.

Chapter Four: Living Differently

1. Matthew 5:16.

2. Matthew 19:16-22.

3. Matthew 22:37-40.

4. Matthew 23:8-12.

5. Matthew 25:34-40.

6. Matthew 5–7.

7. John 2:17.

8. This chapter does not include an analysis of fellowship since I do not have a good body of data on that component of our lives and ministry.

9. The thirteen items were: the Bible is totally accurate in all of its teachings; Satan is a symbol of evil, not a living being; a good person will earn a place in heaven; Jesus committed sins; all religious faiths teach the same lessons; the Holy Spirit is a symbol of God's presence or power but is not a living entity; after He was crucified and died, Jesus Christ did not return to life physically; the Bible teaches that God helps those who help themselves; all people will experience the same outcome after death, regardless of their religious beliefs; some sins cannot be forgiven by God; angels exist and influence people's lives; the universe was originally created by God; the whole idea of sin is outdated. For further information on this research, see "Americans' Bible Knowledge Is in the Ballpark, But Often Off Base," *Barna Update,* July 12, 2000, accessible on the Barna Research Web site (http://www.barna.org).

10. For a more extensive discussion of moral truth and how the United States—and especially the Christian church—

has caved in on absolute truth, see George Barna and Mark Hatch, *Boiling Point* (Ventura, Calif.: Regal, 2001).

11. This principle was first communicated to us in Genesis 12:1-3 but constitutes a common thread of Jesus' teaching as well.

12. There are three types of averages: a mean, a median, and a mode. The average referred to here is the median, which means that if we listed the total amounts donated by people during the year to their churches in order from least to most, the amount donated that falls exactly in the middle of that range would be the median. We use the median rather than the mean (which is derived by adding the total value of all contributions and dividing by the number of donors) to avoid distortions due to extreme amounts at either the high or low ends of the scale.

13. For additional information about giving patterns, read "Evangelicals Are the Most Generous Givers, But Fewer Than 10% of Born-Again Christians Give 10% to Their Church," *Barna Update,* April 5, 2000, accessible on the Barna Research Web site (http://www.barna.org).

14. For more information about spiritual gifts, read Romans 12:6-8; 1 Corinthians 12:1-11,28-31; Ephesians 4:11-13; and 1 Peter 4:10-11.

15. The identification of a twenty-point difference as the cutoff for recognizing truly significant attitudes, values, behaviors, and beliefs is not as arbitrary as it may seem. It is based on the recognition that the average American has five people with whom he or she has a close, personal relationship. Consequently, a person is most likely to be influenced by the thoughts and deeds of those people. When one out of the five individuals in a person's circle of influencers (20 percent) expresses a different viewpoint or demonstrates a behavior, the person is likely to notice that distinction. When two out of the five influencers (40 percent) think or live differently, it will have a substantial impact on the person's personal choices. We originally found this to be pertinent among teenagers and have since seen that the same principle is at work in the lives of adults. Certainly, people are influenced in many different ways and by different types of people. However, the most significant and lasting influences relate to personal relationships with trusted friends and family members.

Chapter Five: How We Got Here— and Where We Go From Here

1. Proverbs 22:6.

2. Revelation 3:15-16.

3. Reading the works of these men would be helpful, even though their focus is upon business and profitability. Take

a look at James Collins and Jerry Porras, *Built to Last* (New York: Harper Business, 1994), and Tom Peters, *The Tom Peters Seminar* (New York: Vintage Books, 1994).

Chapter Seven: Five Models of Effective Discipleship

1. To read more about Pantego Bible Church, visit the church's Web site at http://www.pantego.org.

2. Fellowship Bible Church of Little Rock can be explored on the Web at http://www.fbclr.com.

3. Perimeter Church has a very extensive description of its process on its Web site, http://www.perimeter.org.

4. The Fellowship Bible Church North Web site is http://www.fbcnorth.org.

5. The Web site for North Coast Church is http://www.northcoastchurch.com.

6. These descriptions are based on my observations and interpretations of each church's model. I have done my best to comprehend these models through combinations of interviews, site visits, reading materials, and other input. It is entirely possible that I may have inadvertently misinterpreted something or missed some elements of any given model. The fault for such oversights is mine alone.

BIBLIOGRAPHY

Arn, Win, and Charles Arn. *The Master's Plan for Making Disciples.* Grand Rapids, Mich.: Baker, 1998.

Barna, George. *The Habits of Highly Effective Churches.* Ventura, Calif.: Regal, 2000.

————. *Re-Churching the Unchurched.* Ventura, Calif.: Issachar Resources, 2000.

————. *The Second Coming of the Church.* Nashville: Word, 1998.

————, and Mark Hatch. *Boiling Point.* Ventura, Calif.: Regal, 2001.

Blaikie, Graham, et. al. *Discovering Intimacy with God.* The Discovery Series, Book 2. Plano, Tex.: Center for Church Based Training, 1996.

Bridges, Jerry. *The Pursuit of Holiness.* Colorado Springs: NavPress, 1978.

Bruce, A. B. *The Training of the Twelve.* Grand Rapids, Mich.: Kregel, 1998.

Carr, Brad. *Discovering How to Share Your Faith.* The Discovery Series, Book 4. Plano, Tex.: Center for Church Based Training, 1996.

————, et. al. *Discovering Your Role in God's Family.* The Discovery Series, Book 3. Plano, Tex.: Center for Church Based Training, 1996.

Coleman, Robert. *The Master Plan of Discipleship.* Old Tappan, N.J.: Revell, 1987.

Colson, Charles, and Nancy Pearcey. *How Now Shall We Live?* Wheaton, Ill.: Tyndale, 1999.

Eims, Leroy. *The Lost Art of Disciple Making.* Grand Rapids, Mich.: Zondervan, 1987.

Hoffecker, W. Andrew, ed. *Building A Christian World View.* Volume 1. Phillipsburg, N.J.: Presbyterian and Reformed, 1986.

Hull, Bill. *The Disciple-Making Church.* Grand Rapids, Mich.: Revell, 1990.

Jones, Jeffrey, et. al. *Discovering the Christian Life.* The Discovery Series, Book 1. Plano, Tex.: Center for Church Based Training, 1996.

ACKNOWLEDGMENTS

This report is a collaborative effort. I designed and analyzed the research and wrote the text of this book. My colleagues at Barna Research implemented the research process. My family and friends prayed for me during the intensive writing process. The church leaders who are modeling discipleship shared their experiences and insights with us. The thousands of people we interviewed about their faith and their discipleship experiences provided invaluable understanding of where the church is today and of where we need to go. Take any of these pieces away from the puzzle and it ceases to be a puzzle—merely an incomplete collection of items that have no apparent purpose.

Let me specifically thank some individuals whose efforts on this project deserve special recognition. David Kinnaman kept Barna Research running during my absence and has been an incredible colleague to work with. I could not have abandoned the company without his so masterfully calling the shots. Rachel Ables was a constant source of encouragement and enthusiasm, supportive to the hilt. The other members of the core team pulled their weight and then some during this period; they are a privilege to minister with as we strive to help the church. Thanks are due to Pam Jacob, Jill Kinnaman, Carmen Moore, Sarah Polley, Irene Robles, Celeste Rivera, and Meg Wells.

Julie Carobini provided very helpful editorial advice for the initial edition of this book. Kim Wilson expertly managed the affairs of The Barna Institute, one of our ministry ventures, while I researched and wrote this book. The team at WaterBrook Press helped to refine the book for this current edition.

Once again, my family has been a source of joy, strength, and encouragement during the book-birthing process. They endured the required sacrifices without complaining and shared the joy of achievement upon the book's completion. To my girls—my wife, Nancy, and my daughters, Samantha and Corban—you know that you are the best! May this book produce spiritual fruit that more than repays your investment in me and in this process.

As a disciple of Jesus, I must save the greatest praise and thanks for Him. He directs my paths, He opens doors, He strengthens me, and He loves me. I pray that this book will be an act of worship and service that He finds worthy of His name. And I pray that my life will be worthy of that name too.

ABOUT GEORGE BARNA

George Barna is the president of the Barna Research Group, Ltd., a marketing research firm located in Ventura, California. The company specializes in conducting primary research for Christian ministries and nonprofit organizations. Since its inception in 1984, Barna Research has served several hundred parachurch ministries and numerous churches, in addition to various nonprofit and for-profit organizations.

Barna is a prolific author. His most recent works include *The Power of Team Leadership, Growing True Disciples, Boiling Point,* and *Real Teens.* Past works include bestsellers such as *The Frog in the Kettle, The Second Coming of the Church, User Friendly Churches, Marketing the Church,* and *The Power of Vision.* Several of his books have received national awards. He has also written for numerous periodicals and has published more than two dozen syndicated reports on a variety of topics related to ministry. His work is frequently cited as an authoritative source by the media.

Barna is also widely known for his intensive, research-based seminars for church leaders. He is a popular speaker at ministry conferences around the world and has taught at several universities and seminaries. He has served as a pastor of a large, multi-ethnic church and has served on several boards of directors.

After graduating summa cum laude in sociology from Boston

College, Barna earned two master's degrees from Rutgers University. He also received a doctorate from Dallas Baptist University.

He lives with his wife, Nancy, and their two daughters, Samantha and Corban, in southern California. He enjoys spending time with his family, writing, reading, playing basketball and guitar, relaxing on the beach, and visiting bookstores.

ABOUT THE BARNA
RESEARCH GROUP, LTD.

———◆◆◆———

The Barna Research Group, Ltd. (BRG) is a full-service marketing research company in Ventura, California. BRG has been providing information and analysis regarding cultural trends, ministry practices, marketing and business strategy, fundraising, worldviews, and leadership since 1984. The vision of the company is to provide Christian ministries with current, accurate, and reliable information in bite-sized pieces and at affordable prices to facilitate effective and strategic decision making.

BRG conducts both quantitative and qualitative research using a variety of data collection methods, with particular emphasis on the application of the results. The company conducts more research within the Christian community than any other organization in the United States and regularly releases reports describing its findings regarding the values, attitudes, lifestyles, religious beliefs, and religious practices of adults and teenagers as well as the current state of churches. That information is also accessible through the seminars, books, Web site, and tapes produced by BRG.

To access many of the findings of BRG, visit the company's Web site at http://www.barna.org. You will have access to the free bimonthly reports *(The Barna Update)* published on the site, a data archive that provides current statistics in relation to forty aspects of ministry and lifestyle, the various resources produced by George

Barna and the Barna Research Group, and information about upcoming seminars as well as the firm's research activities. If you wish to receive *The Barna Update* by e-mail every two weeks, you may sign up for that free service on the home page of the site.

To contact the Barna Research Group, call 805-658-8885 or write to 5528 Everglades Street, Ventura, CA 93003.